FREE INDEED

With all my
Love in Jesus
Ron Sims

The author has made every effort to ensure all details in *Free Indeed* are correct. If there are any queries please contact the author c/o Marshall Pickering.

Also by Ron Sims:
Flying Free

FREE INDEED

by

Ron Sims

Collins

Marshall Pickering

William Collins Sons & Co. Ltd
London ● Glasgow ● Sydney ● Auckland
Toronto ● Johannesburg

First published in Great Britain in 1990 by Marshall
Pickering

Marshall Pickering is an imprint of
Collins Religious Division,
part of the Collins Publishing Group
8 Grafton Street, London W1X 3LA

Printed and bound in Great Britain by
Cox & Wyman Ltd, Reading, Berks.

CONTENTS

Acknowledgements

Over the past four years my family have had the privilege of being part of the family of God at the King's Church, Aldershot; my work is now an associated ministry of that church. Much of the content of this book has grown, as has my ministry, as a direct result of the teaching, love and encouragement I have received from the leadership and members. I want to thank three people in particular who have given me great encouragement in the preparation of this book. First, my secretary, Rita Horton, for the professional way she has logged and kept records of my ministry, and also organised the administrative side of it. Also a special thank you to Sandy Stockwell, who is personal assistant to Derek Brown, the leader of King's Church, for typing up the manuscript. Thirdly, I want to thank Dr Richard Whitehouse who has spent hours with me putting this book together, and has helped me in many ways over the years.

Finally, my love and gratitude to my wife Maureen, and sons Graham, Michael and David, for their never-ending love, encouragement, understanding and support in the ministry that God has called me to.

I love you all with the love of Jesus.

Ron Sims

1. New Beginnings

After washing and towelling myself down, I walked from the bathroom to the bedroom and began to change into more presentable clothes. I was due to speak at a local church that evening. As I buttoned up my shirt and straightened my tie I looked round for my wallet. It was nowhere to be seen.

"That's funny," I muttered to myself, "I could have sworn I left it on the bed." Where could it be? "Maureen," I shouted downstairs, "have you seen my wallet?"

"You left it on the bed," came the reply. That was what I had thought too. I remembered tossing it onto the bed when I had come in, so where could it be?

"The boys' friend!" I thought. "Oh no, how careless of me." My sons had had a friend in earlier and they had been chatting upstairs. I called the boys in.

"Have you seen my wallet?" I said accusingly.

"No," they both said, looking hurt that I should suspect them.

"Think," I said, "it's important. There was over a hundred pounds in it. Did your friend come out of your room?"

"Yes, Dad, he went out to the bathroom."

"That's it," I said. "He's stolen my money. Get him back over here." The boy lived nearby, on our estate. By the time he returned to our house I was livid. I knew he had stolen the money, but there was no way I could prove it.

"You're lucky you didn't try that on a few years ago," I snapped at him. "I would have wiped the floor with you. As it is, you had better know that is God's money, not just mine. He will see that you are dealt with. I can't afford to lose it, but I am not taking this any further. If you return the money, nothing more will be said. If you don't, I want to warn you, you are treading on spiritually dangerous ground."

The young man left, looking scared but still not admitting to anything, and when he had gone my anger subsided. I needed to ask forgiveness for some of the direction which my anger had taken, but that was soon dealt with. "Thank God this didn't happen a few years back," I reflected. "Things have certainly changed in that respect."

Things had changed not only in that respect but in many others. Only six or eight years before an incident like that would have provoked me to physical violence. But then I was a villain, a crook with a history of violence and exploitation. Now everything was different. Christ had made all the difference to my life.

I thought back to the months following my last two massive heart attacks. Twice I had been pronounced clinically dead, but I had survived, brought back from the dead by prayer, and I wasn't even a Christian then. That was what had set me thinking so that when Trefor Jones, the local Baptist minister, gave me some literature I was ready to respond.

From the moment I invited Christ into my life, things began to change. Within weeks Maureen saw the changes in me and she too became a Christian, to be followed later by our three sons.

We had thrown ourselves wholeheartedly into the life of the local Baptist church and began to reach out to others. The results were dramatic, but not entirely welcomed by this little village congregation. Soon we were forced to look around for a more congenial spiritual home. Through God's guidance we ended up as members of the King's Church, Aldershot, a few miles from Hartley Wintney where we live. We were glad to enjoy the exuberant worship and the excellent teaching ministry. It was here that we, as a family, were to receive a thorough grounding in the basic principles of the Christian life. Here, too, we experienced a searching inflow of the Holy Spirit, which was to make a remarkable difference to our lives.

One thing we knew from the beginning: if Christ had set us free from the sordid and vicious lifestyle we had known, then he could do it for anyone. We couldn't help but share our new-found experience with those around us. Not all of them welcomed it, but some responded. Even one or two who had been involved with us in the pornography racket surrendered their lives to Christ, with far-reaching consequences.

Gradually, invitations came in from churches and other Christian groups for me to share the dramatic story of my conversion. I was pulled into public preaching almost without being aware of what was happening. I sometimes wonder, if I had known what lay ahead, whether I would have been so eager!

Fortunately, God rarely reveals the whole of the future to us in one flash of revelation. He prefers to lead us step by step into the freedom he has planned for us.

2. The Anointing

The Lord's purposes are wonderful, but the ways in which he works them can certainly be strange. God brought two men thousands of miles so that I could receive the power and authority to fulfil the mission to which he was calling me. Both of these men came from the same church in South Africa. Neither knew that the other had met me, yet they told me substantially the same thing!

On a bright spring morning in April 1985, Maureen and I had joined other members of our church to travel up to London. We were due to meet my friend Mike Pusey and his wife Margaret. Mike was then founder-pastor of King's Church, Aldershot. He had previously introduced us to the work of Reinhard Bonnke, a German evangelist based in South Africa, and now he had arranged for us to hear him preaching at the Royal Albert Hall.

I had seen a couple of video recordings of Bonnke's work in Africa. He uses a massive 32,000-seater tent requiring ten articulated trucks to move it around. Wherever he goes, huge crowds gather and there are significant demonstrations of the Holy Spirit's power evident in salvation and healing.

On the way up to London on the train I wondered, idly, what we were going to see. As we arrived outside the Royal Albert Hall I was surprised to see the crowds gathered. Daffodils in Hyde Park nodded their heads in the spring breeze and a replica of what looked like Stephenson's Rocket puffed up and down. We had plenty of time to watch it as we had to queue for one and a half hours to get into the hall.

The meetings were part of the Elim Church's national conference and many of the people gathered seemed to know each other. But I did not join in the animated conversations, for I was preoccupied. As we wound our way up the stairs into the auditorium I was experiencing mixed emotions. I wanted to analyse, understand and observe the secrets of this man's dynamic power in God. Maybe there was something I could learn from him.

The buzz of talk died down as the meeting got under way. It was lively, but quite restrained compared with the worship in my home church. Still, it was interesting to be in an even larger crowd worshipping the Lord. Reinhard Bonnke took the microphone and began to preach. He spoke with a thick German accent, but his forthrightness and clarity of presentation were impressive. At the conclusion of his message we saw people saved and miraculously healed. I was taken aback by the man's tremendous boldness and power in the Holy Spirit. When I heard him say, "There are some people here who know the Lord has called them into a special ministry of evangelism and healing in the power of the Holy Spirit, to go into the whole world and preach the gospel" I was immediately gripped by the power of the Holy Spirit. "Please come out now," he said. The next thing I knew I was jumping over seats to be prayed for.

Reinhard Bonnke prayed over me and told me that God had called me into a special ministry. "You will be used to bring salvation to many and healing to others," he said. "Go and pray for that lady over there." I did and, to my surprise, she fell to the floor under the power of God's anointing.

As we left the hall I felt as though my feet weren't touching the floor! I felt recharged and elated, but my mind was still full of questions. Was the man just saying those things or was it real? Did he say that to everybody who responded or was it just for me? Deep down I felt sure it was a particular revelation of God for me. And I realised that if God was saying that, then it must mean that I was going to live.

On the train home Maureen and I discussed what had taken place. She said that she had always known that something supernatural had taken place at the time of my last heart attack, over and above my healing. She believed that God had spared my life for a very special purpose. Maureen has constantly been a source of encouragement to me, even when I am down. In the front-line of the battle, God's ministers often get battered and discouraged. What a privilege and blessing it is to have a partner alongside who is cool-headed and sees issues clearly. Now, although I was by no means discouraged, I needed the confirmation of what Maureen had to say.

A few weeks later Ray McCauley visited our church in Aldershot. Ray is the pastor of the church in Johannesburg of which Reinhard Bonnke was then a member. He was a professional body builder and a former Mr Universe before he was converted. Now he is more usefully occupied building the body of Christ! When he came to the Lord, Ray was not content just to fill a pew: he wanted to get out and serve his God. When he first began to preach, he could only read hesitantly. In fact he used to ask his wife to get up and read the Scripture passage for him before he preached. Knowing there facts about Ray was a great encouragement to me. Even before we met, there were many points of contact between us.

During his meeting, Ray pointed to me and called me out to the front. I had never met the man before and he certainly had not talked to anyone about me. He prayed over me and prophesied that I was to receive a special anointing to evangelise and to bring healing to many. A power I had never before experienced went through me. I felt as if I was literally on fire and I collapsed under the power of God's Spirit.

Since these two men of God prayed over me I have received a great spirit of boldness and an anointing to lay hands on the sick and see them healed. I no longer have any difficulties about praying for people, no matter what their illness, great or small. The Psalmist speaks of a God, "who pardons all your iniquities, who heals all your diseases" (Ps. 103.3). Jesus died for every sickness in my body and soul and he himself said that those who believe "will lay hands on the sick and they will recover" (Mark 16.18). I have never had difficulties with passages such as that. I have simply believed that Jesus cannot lie.

I believe that the Holy Spirit cannot lie because he *is* holy. I don't understand people who claim that some of the Bible isn't true. Even some conservative evangelical Christians, while claiming to believe the whole Bible, do not practise some of it and relegate other parts to the past. They are living in practical unbelief.

I believe that this is why so many people do not experience the fulness of being a Christian. Although it is true that particular people are anointed to receive special gifts of healing from the Holy Spirit, anyone can pray for the sick. We can all lay hands on the sick, not only the Reinhard Bonnkes or Ray McCauleys. If we claim the promises that Jesus extends to us in the Bible we will still see miracles, signs and wonders. They are the evidence of the Kingdom of God. After all, the New Testament is the last will and testament of Jesus. He is the only person who ever made out a will, died and then rose from the dead to make sure the provisions of that will were kept!

*

In a dream, a few days later, the Lord said to me, "I have anointed you, you have received power from on high. Not only will you testify, but you will preach and at the appointed time you will be used in the revival that is coming. Do not look for places to go, I will send you where you are to go. I will open my doors to you. Your ministry is only starting. In three years you will see the fruits of your labour. Go preach my gospel, go into prison and set the prisoners free."

Until this time, my evangelistic activities were largely confined to sharing my own story of what God had done for me. I told my audiences that if he could do it for me, with my background, he could do it for anybody. I would then make an appeal for people to respond to the Lord. Many did, but I knew that further developments needed to take place in order for me to move effectively within this new anointing from God. A ministerial friend began to show me how I could use the elements of my life story to illustrate biblical truths. It was from this base that I began to preach, rather than just repeat my testimony.

The Lord told me not to look for places to go, and we have never yet invited ourselves to preach. Maureen and I have travelled all over the country. We have made countless, exhausting journeys in our battered old Chevette, through the length and breadth of the land, but everywhere we have gone has been by invitation.

Many of these invitations have come from folk we have never even heard of, let alone met. Church leaders from distant parts of the country have contacted me by telephone or letter requesting a visit to preach in their area. Some of these appointments have come through the network of the Full Gospel Business Men's Fellowship International.

FGBMFI is an interesting organisation. Set up in California by a dairy farmer named Demos Shakarian, it now has local chapters all over the world. The idea behind it is simple. Many men tend to think of Christianity as a woman's affair and are inhibited from going to church. So Demos Shakarian received the vision to invite men to a cafeteria or restaurant for a meal and to hear another businessman tell the story of his faith in Christ. The interpretation of the term "businessman" is wide. Anyone from the plumber to the bank manager may attend! The rules are also simple. Christians are expected to invite non-Christian friends or colleagues to a meal and to hear a speaker. Speakers are not allowed to preach, purely to give their testimony. This pattern of men hearing other men relate their Christian faith to their business life has been the means of thousands finding Christ and being channelled into the Church.

Because I was known to have a dramatic testimony, invitations poured in from all over the country. At these meetings we have seen many people come to Jesus. Many testimonies of healings and miracles, signs and wonders have been recorded, all to the glory of God. On two such visits to the Tunbridge Wells chapter we saw sixty people making a confession of faith in Jesus. At one meeting alone, in Portsmouth, twenty-two came to Christ including five policemen, one an inspector.

Some churches see the FGBMFI chapters as a threat. I know that some Christians have treated them as alternative churches, or have gone to get a monthly spiritual shot in the arm, while remaining complacently in a dead church. But this is not their purpose. The FGBMFI should always be an evangelistic arm of the Body of Christ and work with and for the benefit of the local churches, not as an alternative to them. The real vision is to invite to the dinners people of every class and denomination, the unsaved as well as the saved, to see the unsaved won for

Christ and the saved baptised in the Holy Spirit. Then they are returned, or introduced to, a local church, preferably one that is on fire for the Lord and where they will grow.

Clearly FGBMFI was a suitable platform for a testimony ministry such as mine was originally, but it has also led to other things. From these meetings I have often received invitations to churches as a result of an FGBMFI member recommending me to his church leaders. Of course, in the church context I am not confined to giving my testimony and it was here that my preaching ministry began to take shape.

My first book *Flying Free* was by now widely circulated in the Christian bookshops, and we received many reports of people finding the Lord through it. Over a hundred people have written in to say that its pages were the means of their conversion, and the book itself brought in many more invitations to preach. Gradually, as a reputation became established and people saw the fruits of the new anointing, I was being asked to take missions of up to a week's duration. All of the time we were witnessing conversions and remarkable healings.

With a handful of churches, a relationship has been established and I have been asked to return several times. Usually, these have been churches where the pastor or leaders have encouraged me and, in turn, my visits have built something of numerical growth into their churches. In some cases, churches have come into remarkable growth as a result of this close interaction between evangelist and pastors.

One of these pastors is Richard Whitehouse, whom we first met at a leaders' conference at High Leigh Conference Centre, organised by my own church leaders. He was then pioneering a new church in the London borough of Hounslow. Richard is an ex-academic and I am an ex-convict, but despite the great difference in our backgrounds, somehow we hit it off straight away. Not long after that, Richard and his leaders invited me to preach at a short mission split between two centres in the borough, Heston and Feltham.

Although the meetings weren't particularly well attended, God did some remarkable things. Not least was the healing of two drug addicts who had already made a commitment to Christ. I prayed for them and they were completely delivered of their addiction without suffering any withdrawal symptoms. When they turned up at a later meeting we almost didn't recognise them. Gone was the old hippy-type gear but, more importantly, their faces were transformed.

One of the church members, who is a nurse, had fractured her leg in a motorbike accident. Richard had brought her in a wheelchair as her leg was heavily plastered. During the worship she felt a warmth go through her body and she stood up and walked. I have a copy of the subsequent X-ray which shows no fracture site, although it is clearly present in the previous one.

A friendship developed with Richard and his leaders, and in 1986 they invited me and the family to join them on their church holiday in South Wales. This led to developments none of us ever dreamed of. As a result, Richard is now pioneering churches in South Wales where his ministry and teaching input have been readily accepted in many parts, and together we have shared in many outreaches.

One of the consequences of the Hounslow connection was that I was invited to a mission at the Bell Farm Church in West Drayton. This church is an amalgam of the West Drayton Christian Fellowship and a Shaftesbury Mission Church. The leaders were friends of Richard and that was how I came to get the invitation.

During the three days of the mission in October 1987 I based my preaching on the themes "Jesus our Saviour", "Jesus our Healer" and "Jesus our Deliverer". About fifteen people were converted, there were healings, and youngsters were delivered from drug abuse and the effects of involvement in the occult movement.

The most memorable event was the healing of a twenty-seven-year-old married man who was in a wheelchair, suffering from a spinal wasting disease. He also had a tumour, twice the size of my fist, growing below the back of his neck. After prayer this man took ten steps, the first for a very long time. By the third night the tumour had completely disappeared and not only was he walking totally unaided, but he actually offered to race his wife around the estate, to the amazement of us all!

I know readers may find this difficult to believe; this is most understandable. I was there, I saw it, but I still cannot comprehend it myself. How right Jesus was when he spoke of the hardness of our hearts. Even when he walked this earth confirming the word of God with signs and miracles, people could not accept the evidence that was before them.

This man's wife was heavily involved in the occult, but she too was born again and has cleaned up her life. The Sunday following this meeting, eight converts were baptised by immersion.

One of my earliest experiences of working on an extended mission was with a church in Northampton. I was invited to share a week of outreach meetings with Lewis Houston and his team at the Kingsthorpe Christian Fellowship. The meetings were held in the town hall and were shared with Derek Brown, our pastor, and Trevor and Shirley Martin.

I travelled up to Northampton a couple of days earlier than the rest because I was due to go into a number of schools and had appointments. It was here too that I had my first taste of broadcasting on the local radio. After the radio interview, Lewis and I went off into the local market square and shared Jesus for a number of hours with the people, inviting them to the meetings. The meetings were greatly blessed throughout the week and I was encouraged by the ministry of Trevor and Shirley Martin, as well as Derek, with whom I was more familiar.

We saw miracles, and many people were saved during that week. People were healed from all sorts of diseases: hay fever, bronchitis, cysts, epilepsy, heart conditions and even fear of flying. Many more people were baptised in the Holy Spirit. I was interested to note that Trevor and Shirley came to the meetings having spent time with the Lord and hearing from him what healing miracles he was going to do. Quietly and in a matter-of-fact way they announced what God had told them, and people would respond.

At the meeting where I shared my testimony and preached, twenty-two people gave their lives to the Lord. One of the lessons I learned then was not to judge by outward appearances. That night a couple of hippies were among those who came forward. The girl's hair was dyed all manner of colours and the boy was long-haired and scruffy. My first thought was, "Lord, surely you are not calling these?" I remember going down and asking them what they had come out to the front for, and they said, "We want to give our hearts to the Lord." I asked if they knew what that really meant because I suspected that they were not living a very good life. In fact they were living together, although unmarried. I questioned them further to make sure that they knew what they were doing, and they persisted in saying that they did.

I thought, "Okay, Lord, you know what you're doing," though not believing for one minute that this couple were sincere and genuine converts. So I just prayed for them, as I prayed with all the others, and they left.

It was a tremendous week, but it wasn't until I returned to share with this fellowship again at the invitation of Lewis about three months later that the story was completed. A beautiful black-haired young woman came up to me, very smartly dressed. "Hello, Ron, don't you remember me?" she said. I had to admit I didn't. Then a young man joined her and shook my hand. I was totally amazed when they told me they were the two hippies who had responded on our previous visit.

I just could not believe the transformation. I could not believe they were the same couple. They had changed so much physically, they were unrecognisable. How true is the Scripture that says that if anyone is in Christ they are new creations, old things have gone, everything has become new. I was learning not to be taken in by externals.

I asked them what had happened the night they came forward. They explained that after leaving the meeting they went outside and realised they could not go on living the way they had been. If they were going to live for Jesus they could not continue to live together. Subsequently, the girl decided to go back and live with her parents, and her boyfriend went back to the flat they were sharing to live on his own.

They not only began to clear up their lives spiritually but physically. The gospel isn't just a hope in heaven after you die, it is a matter of healthy living now. This couple went on to ask me to their wedding, as they were getting married in three months' time. That is how great our God is.

The fellowship at Northampton became very close to me. I love them all. Subsequently, I returned there with Derek Brown. I remember on that particular Sunday morning Derek and I were leading the meeting when, for no apparent reason at all, I dropped to my knees and began to cry. We can even pray with tears. I didn't know why I was crying, but I saw that Derek was too, and before long the whole congregation was in tears. Then Derek received a word of knowledge from the Lord. He said, "There are many hurts in this congregation. There is a lot of unforgiveness, a lot of old wounds that need to be cleared up."

This triggered off an unforgettable response. Soon, people were going up to each other, hugging one another, forgiving one another and loving one another. It ended with the congregation presenting Derek and me with a bouquet of flowers each for our wives. Then they stood up and sang, "I love you with the love of the Lord." My tears flowed now for a different reason. How good it is for someone who has felt society's rejection to be so loved and accepted.

Another church with which we have enjoyed a fruitful relationship is the Poplars Christian Fellowship near Worksop. Situated on the Nottinghamshire-Yorkshire borders it is what I call "flat cap and ferret country". The leaders, Derek Wilkinson and Norman Daniels, have big hearts, but they certainly work you hard.

I had a hectic time when I went up to work with them. I think I had about eighteen appointments altogether, including school visits, youth meetings and interviews on Radio Sheffield and Worksop Hospital Radio. I had a tremendous time with these people and part of my heart will always be with them. Like me, they are very simple in their ways and they understand my simple way of sharing the gospel. I stayed at the home of Norman Daniels and, as with every other Christian home I have stayed in, I was accepted and treated as one of the family. In between engagements, Norman, his wife and myself had a great time of sharing and having fellowship together. I was amazed at the price of houses. A three-bedroomed, modernised house at that time sold for £12,000, when at home the same thing would have fetched £50,000. I was made aware of the difference between the wealth of the south and the poverty of some parts of the north.

Some of the folks in the south who think they have got it hard or are missing out on the material things of life should take a trip up north. Then I think many of them would praise God for the blessings they have. But, apart from a harder life and the struggles of living on very limited incomes, these people seem to be full of joy and laughter and ready to share what little they have. It just goes to show that money doesn't buy happiness and nothing can compare with the joy of the Lord. Knowing Jesus is the greatest treasure a person can have.

The last evening of my visit to Worksop ended with a public meeting in the village hall at Carlton. It was packed out with people from all denominations. What a tremendous time we had! The praise and worship was exuberant and after the message people were born again, healed and baptised in the Holy Spirit. It was as though we were experiencing Bible days again. Many lives were changed and even committed Christians entered into a new personal relationship with Jesus.

After the meeting I returned to Norman's home for a meal after which I left for the long journey home. I got back about 3.30 a.m. Norman wanted me to stay the night and travel back the next day, but I couldn't wait to get home and see my wife and family. This is such a change for me. In the old days, I would spend weeks away from my family without a thought. Now, even after a day away from home, I get homesick. Such is the love that Jesus gives, a love I have never known before.

At the time the Lord told me he would send me where I was to go and that he would open doors for me, I was not overloaded with work. From time to time I would be asked out to speak, but I wasn't overworked. Naturally, I interpreted his words to mean that I should go everywhere I was invited. For months I never refused an invitation. Consequently, I was soon rushing up and down the country on a series of one night stands. There was no rhyme or reason to it. One day I might be in Norwich and the next in Portsmouth. Although God had healed me of coronary heart disease I still suffered from angina and the schedule I was following would have been dangerous for a fit man of half my age. I was so keen to do the Lord's will, but I was reaching the point of exhaustion. Maureen and other friends begged me to slow down and the Lord also sent me warning signs, for I would occasionally get twinges of heart pain.

It took me a long time to realise that because the Lord had promised to open doors, this didn't mean that every invitation I received was from him. This began to dawn on me because the dates of some invitations clashed. Clearly, they couldn't all be from the Lord. At the very least, sometimes someone was getting the timing wrong and it wasn't him! I had to learn discernment, through the guidance of the Holy Spirit.

I have had to learn to recognise the Spirit's prompt-ings, not only on when and where, but on how I should preach. Many times I have preached under the influence of the Holy Spirit with no notes. I have done my homework, prepared and put together a message, and then the Lord has said, "Leave it," and I have preached out of my spirit. God has honoured this, but I don't believe I can presume on it. In fact, it has happened more often than not when I have put in the most preparation. Ministering in the power of God's Spirit is no excuse for laziness. The minute we presume on God, he deserts us and leaves us to our own devices.

The Lord showed me the three most powerful verses in the Bible for an evangelist: "I tell you the truth, anyone who has faith in me will do what I have been doing. He will do even greater things than these, because I am going to the Father. And I will do whatever you ask in my name, so that the Son may give glory to the Father. You may ask me for anything in my name, and I will do it" (John 14.12–14). Many ministries fail because people find this Scripture too hard to accept or believe. It is all a question of who gets the glory.

Jesus said everything he did we can do. Do you believe that? This is meant to be the normal Christian life. We can do even greater things than Jesus did because he goes to his Father in heaven and sends us the Holy Spirit. The power force in our ministries is the power that even the twelve disciples were denied until the Day of Pentecost. And with that power we can go and do all the things that Jesus did, and even more. He had only three and a half years of ministry, yet I have met many Christians of as many as twenty-five years' standing who have never led a single soul to Jesus. It is a commission for us all. It is no good making excuses. Jesus said, "Go into all the world and preach the gospel." He commissioned every one of us to share the good news and to lead others to him. But, as I have learned, we will never be able to do it in our own strength. We need the power of the Holy Spirit.

3. Satan's Backyard

The envelope dropped through our letterbox onto the mat. It looked innocent enough – just one of the scores of letters that come through our door every week – but it was to change the direction of my life. It came from Roger Lockwood, minister of an independent Methodist church in Wellingborough, Northamptonshire.

I remembered Roger from one of the leadership conferences sponsored by our church leaders in Aldershot. We had chatted during some of the intervals and had got on pretty well together. Now Roger was inviting me to preach at his church. In the course of the letter he mentioned that the Rev Tom Johns of Wellingborough Youth Custody Centre would like me to go into the prison on the Sunday morning to address the lads there.

I had never forgotten that part of my special commission from the Lord was to go into prisons to set the prisoners free. When I first heard this command from God, I had been very reluctant to accept it. Of course, I had read many times in the Bible where Jesus said, "I was in prison and you never visited me," and how when we Christians ask, "When were you in prison and we never visited you?" the Lord answers, "When you failed to visit one of these my brothers, you failed to visit me." Still, I didn't relish the idea of going back into prisons.

Right until the time I became a Christian I had

suffered with a tremendous fear when anyone banged a door or jangled keys. The memories of prison used to flood back in upon me. Since I had become a Christian the fear had gone, but I was still very wary of reawakening all the hateful memories of the time I had spent in prison. I didn't know if I could face going through those big iron gates, hearing cell doors clanging, keys jangling, and the thud of wardens' boots.

I had tried to plead with the Lord. I didn't want the responsibility or the pressure. "Lord, I can't do it. I am still only young in the faith." But the Lord led me to read these verses of Jeremiah: "'Ah, Sovereign Lord,' I said, 'I do not know how to speak; I am only a child.' But the Lord said to me, 'Do not say, "I am only a child." You must go to everyone I send you to and say whatever I command you. Do not be afraid of them, for I am with you and will rescue you,' declares the Lord" (Jer. 1.6–8).

Jeremiah not only had to visit prisoners, he was put in prison himself for his forthright preaching. After reading this I knew why God had spared my life when I had clinically died twice after suffering several heart attacks. God assured me at that time that this was a special anointing he was giving me. He also assured me that if I left it or abused it he would put me back where he found me: in a hospital coronary unit. He had saved me and called me for a special mission and I was to honour the whole of that commission and honour that anointing and see that he received all the glory. So, after much prayer, I gave my whole life afresh to the Lord. I said, "Okay, Lord, take all of me, keep me humble, do not let me get boastful. Let me give you all the honour and the glory."

The battle had been fought. God's command was clear, but now the real test had come. I felt a cold sweat breaking out down my back. I didn't know how I would react to actually going back into prisons. How would I cope? Clanging cell doors echoed down the corridors of my mind and the memory of the claustrophobic atmosphere of confined spaces made my throat contract. I knew that only God could give me the strength to go back in there.

As always, Maureen was a tower of strength. She just put her arm around me and said, "Don't worry, love, the Lord will give you the strength. The Lord never asks us to do anything that he knows we can't handle and he will give you strength – and his Holy Spirit. You'll manage, don't worry." We prayed and offered it up to the Lord, and I knew I had a peace that would enable me to go into that prison in the power of the Lord.

We travelled to Wellingborough and were met by Roger and his wife, who gave us hospitality for the weekend. The local paper interviewed us, wanting to know about my past life and how I became a Christian, and about Maureen's recent healing from cancer. It was a great opportunity to witness to the reporter.

The next morning we were up bright and early. We had to be in the prison early to get clearance. We drove up to the usual grim building, its high walls topped with barbed wire. The massive main door was opened and we were let in. As the door clanged behind us, we waited nervously in "no man's land" while the warden opened the inside door to the courtyard. There we were met by the Rev Tom Johns, the prison chaplain, and a tremendous man of God.

Over the years Tom has been a living testimony to the power of God in prisons. He used to be an assistant to Noel Proctor, whose book *The Cross Behind Bars* gives an account of his ministry in Strangeways where he regularly sees men come to Christ. Tom also sees men come to know the Lord in Wellingborough

Youth Custody Centre. For Tom, it is not just a job, it is a life's calling. He is a modern-day disciple in that prison. Because he truly loves the Lord, he gives his whole life to the lads, spending many hours over and above the requirements of his job, sitting in the cells, even in the punishment blocks, talking to prisoners about the Lord and trying to show them a different way of life.

Tom greeted me and introduced himself and off we went. Much to my surprise, the unlocking and banging of doors as we progressed down the corridors had no effect on me. The jangling of keys, the clanging of bars, the noise of the heavy boots of the guards on the stone floors, no longer held any terrors for me. Jesus had cleared all the painful memories from my mind.

Tom led Maureen and me into a small room at the back of the chapel, but before we could pray we were disturbed by a blackbird which had somehow got into the room and was flying dementedly around. Tom called in one of the officers to catch it. Every time the officer tried to grab the frightened creature it would fly away and smash itself against the wall, only to flop down again. As the officer dived to pick it up it would get up and fly off again. We watched helplessly as the bird continued to batter itself until it was totally exhausted. Finally, it lay on the floor, unable to move except for the wild beating of its heart. The officer was able to pick it up at last, open the window and push it through the bars.

It was then that the Lord spoke to me and said, "That is what you are in here for. Many of these men in here have been beating themselves against a wall, running away from me. I am sending you in, like that guard, to pick them up and set them free."

This was the first time Maureen had been inside a prison. She had heard a lot about them from me, but it was the first time she had seen for herself. She seemed to take everything in her stride and there was a peace about her that I just couldn't understand. I was later to discover that Jesus had given her a special love for prisoners. Many of them have come to look upon her as a friend, as the kind of woman they all hope one day to marry: the kind of woman they can respect.

Maureen was led off into the chapel where she sat with the governor and his wife while Tom and I prayed and prepared for the meeting. When we entered the small chapel I was amazed to see it totally filled. There were a hundred prisoners present, almost one third of the inmate population, as I learned later. As I looked at the faces before me, tears started to well up in my eyes, and my heart was full. As I looked at those lads I could see myself, not so many years before. I realised how the devil was destroying lives. How true are those words in the Bible, that the devil seeks to rob and destroy. Here were dozens of young men who were throwing their lives away. I couldn't help wondering what was behind each one of those faces, what had gone on in their minds, what had caused their destructive behaviour, what were their backgrounds. I guessed that many of them had similar stories to my own and could relate to my past. I knew that somehow I had to get the message of Jesus through to them. Only Jesus, who came to proclaim freedom for the captives, could set these prisoners free.

After a couple of hymns I stood up to speak. As I rose I spoke inwardly to the Lord: "It's up to you, Lord. Just give me the words and give me the power."

I told the lads that I wasn't a religious nut; I was just a man who had an experience of the Lord. I had been born again and I knew Jesus as my personal Saviour. He was a friend and I wanted to share him with them that morning. I tried to explain that there was a person called the devil and there was a living God, and that it wasn't God but the devil who had put them into prison. A lot of them may have felt they were doing their own thing, but in fact it was the devil who was manipulating their lives and had caused their downfall. Only Jesus could set them free.

I assured them that I was telling them the truth. I had better things to do than to travel hundreds of miles just to tell them a pack of lies. If I wanted to "con" people I would be out there using my abilities to make a fortune, like I used to. The fact was that I had travelled all these miles and wasn't getting paid one penny for it. You don't get paid for prison ministry; there is no money available to pay prison evangelists. But it is an honour and a privilege to be able to go in and share the truths of the gospel with them.

As I told them a bit about my life and what God had done for me, I knew I was speaking with a power and authority that was not my own. At the end of the message, all the prisoners in the chapel spontaneously stood and applauded. This is something which has happened many times since. It is the only outward response they are free to make.

You are not allowed to make an appeal in prisons, so I invited anyone who felt they would like to make a commitment to the Lord to ask for a chaplain's visit. I knew that Tom, with his love and knowledge of the Lord and his understanding of the men, was the right person to lead them through.

Maureen and I were asked to go outside first and wait at the door before the men were lined up and led out. Every one of those lads individually shook our hands as they came out. Many had tears in their eyes. They had been touched, and I knew that it was by the power of God. Some of them went over to Tom and asked for a chaplain's visit. We know that many seeds of salvation were sown that day.

We left to go down to Roger's church. In the morning service we were able to share the wonderful things we had seen in the prison earlier that morning and how God had given me the strength to go in there. I knew then that a new ministry was opening up to me; that I was going to be used by the Lord to go into many prisons.

After the meeting, a woman came up to me and said, "Ron, I wonder if you would pray with me?" She told me that her husband was a prison officer and was not a Christian. In fact he was quite hostile to Christianity. They had many arguments at home about her belief and she felt it was getting to the point where she had almost to choose between God and her husband.

"Can we pray that maybe he was in the meeting this morning and that maybe he heard what you said and that maybe it had some impression on him," she said.

"No," I said, "I never pray for maybes. It says in God's word, 'If two people are agreed about anything in my name, it will be done.'" I told her we would pray that her husband *was* in that meeting and in fact not only did hear what I said, but that this would lead to his salvation.

That night I went again to Roger's church and preached, after which a number of people gave their hearts to the Lord. Many came forward for baptism in the Holy Spirit and many more received healing. There were lots of different sorts of problems to contend with. For the first time ever, I came into contact with demonic activity, but I praise God I knew that "greater is he that is in you than he that is in the world".

As I walked out of the meeting, I noticed Tom Johns at the back so I went over and asked him how things were going. He said, "You really have kept me busy today. I've only just finished in time to get to the meeting. Lots of the lads on the wing are wanting to know more about the Lord and more about what you said. And what is more, I believe one of the prison officers may have given his life to the Lord!"

We heard later that this prison officer had, indeed, committed his life to Christ, despite his previous hostility to Christianity. Roger Lockwood was able to confirm that the officer was the husband of the woman with whom I had prayed.

Travelling home that night I pulled into a lay-by and started to cry. I still couldn't believe that God could choose somebody such as me for his work. I cried out to the Lord, "Lord, I am just not worthy of this." I felt the Lord was saying to me, "My Son believed in you; he believed you were worth it. That is why he died for you. I and I alone choose on whom I place my anointing, and I choose many people that the world would look down upon and despise so that my Son will receive all the glory. You have been obedient in giving my Son the glory. Go and preach the word, stay in my perfect will and I will honour your ministry with signs following."

Maureen and I sang choruses and praise to God all the way home. What a tremendous weekend, what a tremendous experience, what a tremendous God we have! Our faith was built up and our love for one another continued growing.

Doors have now been opened up for me by the Lord to go into many prisons. Peter Chadwick, the director of Prison Christian Fellowship, has become a close personal friend and we have shared meetings together to explain and further the work of Prison Christian Fellowship and to encourage churches to get involved in the prison ministry. Peter is one of those who believe that the Lord has given me a unique ministry to the prisons and prisoners of this country, and the Lord has shown me that he is putting an army together in the devil's backyard, in the hellholes of this country. He is going to raise up mighty men of God from our prisons, and he is already doing it.

All the time I was in prison I never met one Christian, but right now most, if not all, of our prisons have Christians in them, both among the prisoners and the staff. In Ashford Remand Centre there are a number of Christian officers collectively known as the God Squad and they have led many remand prisoners to Jesus. So many prison staff, probation officers and prison workers are getting saved that they have now formed their own fellowship, of which Fred Lemon and myself are members. It is known as the Prison Christian Service Fellowship. They, along with Prison Fellowship, represent a mighty recruiting force for the army of men that the Lord is putting together in the prisons. I feel so humble that the Lord should see fit to anoint me also to go into the prisons of this country over the past three years and win and recruit new members for this spiritual army.

It is a fact that we in Britain today incarcerate more people in prisons than ever before. Most of these are young men discontented and distressed, with a big chip on their shoulders, hatred in their hearts and little or no hope for the future. But God works in mysterious ways his wonders to perform. Today more people are being saved in prisons than ever before. Some prisons see more converts than many of our churches. The main reason for this is that they are receiving the full gospel message of Jesus. Many of the chaplains in prisons today are spirit-filled men of God, who see their position as a spiritual vocation. Many of them put in hours of extra work and, along with Christian governors, they encourage people like myself, Fred Lemon, Brian Greenaway, Rita Nightingale and other full-time evangelists and prominent speakers to come in and share the good news of Jesus with the prisoners.

Add to this the many Prison Christian Fellowship groups that visit prisons throughout the country with musical groups, mid-week Bible studies and other activities, and you begin to see the miracle that God is pursuing. The Lord did a similar thing in Old Testament times, when David was in exile. First Samuel chapter 22 verse 2 says, "And everyone in debt, or distress or discontented gathered to him and he became a commander over them. And there were with them about four hundred men." David gathered an army of outcasts who became the very men who took Israel, and the Lord blessed them until David became the greatest ever king of Israel. The commander of the army that is being put together by ministries in our prisons today is Jesus Christ. Jehovah Sabaoth is one of God's names in the Bible: it means "Lord of hosts". The dictionary definition of *hosts* is "heavenly or earthly armies", and Jesus is captain of the hosts of the Lord.

I find it a privilege to live in a time when God is about to work in a way never known before, and an even greater privilege to be one of the many servants that he is going to use to bring this about. If someone had told me some twenty years ago, when I was in prison, that one day God was going to call me to be an evangelist, I would have taken it as a joke. The thought that I would return to prison many, many more times, not as a convicted criminal, but as a free man preaching the good news of Jesus to the convicts and even to the men I used to hate – the prison officers and staff – would have been laughable. But that is exactly what has happened. Nothing is impossible for our God. Yes, I really do love the prison officers and the rest of the staff. It is funny, but since I have been a Christian the people I used to hate the most I love and respect the most. It is Jesus' way to change hatred to love.

One poignant memory is of my return visit to Wellingborough Youth Custody Centre. After the service an older prison officer came up to me and shook my hand with tears in his eyes. "Ron," he said, "You won't remember me, but many years ago I used to lock you up. What I have witnessed in this chapel this morning is a miracle. I am shortly retiring and I want to be used in some way to help these lads." How can people doubt the power of God when you witness things such as these?

Jesus has given me a real love towards the prison staff, and whenever I speak to the inmates in a prison I tell them that they shouldn't hate the officers in charge of them, but should love them. This often raises a snigger from prisoners and officers alike, but I tell them the officers have a thankless job. They are people with families and homes that they have to leave every day to come in and look after people who hate them and sneer at them. Prisoners may be doing a few years, but these men are doing life. Why do they do it? Thank God that they do because if they didn't the alternative would be for prisoners to be put up against a wall and shot.

It is a hard message, but before you can show them the love of Jesus you have to show them the need for Jesus. Many times I tell them, "When I have finished speaking to you I will be going out free to my wife and family, and you will be going back to your cells, locked away as a prisoner. Not only as a prisoner of society, but also a prisoner of Satan." Then I tell them how Jesus can change their situation, as he changed mine. I tell them, "Any mug can get a gun and pull off a job, make a few quid and be popular with the boys, but it takes a real man to take up the Bible, the sword of the Lord, and follow Jesus, and it won't make you popular with your mates."

I tell them that Jesus died for the worst and there was a special place in his heart for criminals. The last man to accept Jesus when he was on this earth was a criminal just like them. He was put on a cross at the side of Jesus and in the last moments of his life he said to Jesus, "Remember me when you come into your Father's Kingdom." What was Jesus' answer to him? "Today you will be with me in Paradise."

I tell the prisoners that Jesus is putting together an army in the prisons and I ask, "Who wants to sign up?" And through the power of God's Holy Spirit, many commit their lives to Jesus. A lost soul won for Jesus is the greatest miracle there is, but when a man in prison, in the depths of hell, is set free and commits his life to Jesus I believe it is the miracle of miracles. I have seen many, many prisoners come to Jesus in prison, all over the country, in every prison I have been in. I am blessed to know that many other prisoners whom I have never met have come to Jesus through reading my book *Flying Free*.

When men in prison commit their lives to Christ they face ridicule and abuse, often of a physical nature. It is no fun to be jostled and punched for your faith. Some men have had their food spat on or urinated on because they make a stand for Jesus. No wonder they come out strong in the faith, for they must either sink or swim. The pity is that when they come out, they often do not find the churches as firm or supportive as the Christian staff in the prisons they have left. They continue to face rejection and ridicule when they come out of prison, and unfortunately Christians sometimes join in. It is sad when ignorance and intolerance blind people to the unprecedented movement of God that is taking place in Satan's backyard.

Since that first visit to Wellingborough, I have witnessed more miraculous events in prisons than it is possible to record here, but I would like to share a few of the more memorable ones.

Jeff Bird, Northern Co-ordinator for Prison Fellowship, went with me to Sudbury Prison where we took an afternoon service. This is an open prison where men are sent when they are nearing the end of a long-term sentence. In this service there were no officers in attendance, and after my message I felt the Lord was prompting me to have an "altar call". I knew this was not permitted in prison, but the message from the Lord persistently repeated, "Have an altar call." It was as though he wouldn't have it any other way. There were no officers there to stop me, so I made an appeal.

I asked the prisoners to give their lives to the Lord publicly, then and there, in front of their mates. And the miracle happened – nine men did exactly that. Can you imagine what courage that takes? Only under the conviction of the Holy Spirit and the power of God was it possible for those men to do such a thing.

My visit to Stoke Heath Youth Custody Centre along with the prison chaplain, Roy Hater, was another victory for Jesus. We saw six lads give their hearts to Jesus, followed by five more a couple of weeks later. But by far the greatest miracle I have so far witnessed in a prison in a single day was my visit to Rochester Prison with Maureen and the chaplain, Rev Richard Winterbottom. On that day twenty-six inmates made a confession of faith, and several of the staff were touched by the power of God.

One of the most remarkable sequences of events led to the conversion of a very important prisoner incarcerated in Pentonville Gaol. So significant was this man's salvation that it even received attention from the national press, albeit somewhat cynical attention. Initially, it had nothing to do with prison other than the fact that the story began in the town of Winchester, where I had served one of my own prison sentences years before. However, apart from past associations, there were no thoughts of prison in my mind as I travelled down to take a special service at Stanmore Evangelical Church.

The pastor, Greg Haslam, had asked me to preach at very short notice and as I motored towards Winchester with Maureen, we had no idea what to expect. Greg himself wasn't too sure what reaction to expect from his people. He wasn't sure how many would come, if any. I told him, "Well, we've done all we can. Now the rest is up to God," and we prayed together before going into the church. God was certainly in control; more and more people began to arrive until the church was nearly full to capacity.

I knew that this was God's time for this place and a sense of his anointing was heavily upon me as I preached. Many surrendered their lives to Christ; others came forward to receive the fullness of the Holy Spirit and to know boldness in witnessing for Christ; others came for healing.

On the edge of the group of people who made a first-time commitment was a rather sad-looking woman. Tall and slim, with short dark hair, she was elegantly dressed and yet I noticed that she seemed troubled. A few days later, I learned that this woman was Maria Herbage, the wife of the well-known international financier, Alex Herbage. Alex was at that time in Pentonville Prison awaiting trial on fraud charges. Severe changes came about in Ria's life as a result of her husband's situation. In the time we have known her she has had to give up her jewellery and eventually lost their palatial home, Sutton Scotney Manor. Coming from a well-to-do German background, Ria was used to society life, but she eventually had to go to work as a secretary with Hampshire County Council in order to make ends meet.

Ria has borne all of these reversals of fortune with a quiet dignity. In the midst of adversity she has managed to stand firm for Christ. Indeed, on one occasion she shared with me how she was struck by genuine Christian friendship when she had nothing. In her days of plenty she was never entirely sure whether people valued her or her possessions. Apart from the deep distress of her husband's situation and her grief for him, Ria testifies that she has never been so fulfilled as she has been since Christ found her and called her to be his child.

I gave Ria Herbage a copy of *Flying Free*, and she passed it on to Alex in prison. He read it avidly and soon, through her, he asked me to visit him in Pentonville.

Since the fraud charges against him involved millions of pounds, Alex Herbage was held in Pentonville on remand for almost two years. Eventually, all charges against him in this country were dropped and he was extradited to face charges in America.

By the time I went up to Pentonville to meet him, Alex was a pale shadow of the man he had been. As he lumbered towards me, hand extended, his clothes sagged on his still-large frame. Lines of mental anguish were etched into his face. I could see that he was being destroyed mentally and physically as his dignity was stripped from him.

Many times, on subsequent visits, Alex has come from his cell and fallen into my arms, hugging me and crying like a baby as all the hurts have risen to the surface. During these visits I was able to encourage him to put his faith, hope and future into the hands of the Almighty God and Alex is now a Christian. Jesus is bringing about many changes in his life and he says that if he had not been confined to prison he would never have given Jesus a second thought.

Since beginning the prison ministry I have developed a relationship not only with prison officers, but with the other group that I once regarded as my enemies – the police force.

Recently, I met up with an old opponent from the past. He was a police officer in Basingstoke CID when I was one of the local villains with the mob. He had put a few of my old mates away and had been one of my worst enemies. He came up to me when I was taking a meeting at Farnham and said, "I heard about you and I was a bit sceptical, but what I have just seen and heard from your mouth is a miracle. You would never believe this was the old Ron Sims." He went on to tell me that he had recently become a Christian himself and had experienced a new life in Jesus.

I can tell you, he had been a real hard nut like me, only on the opposite side. Now here we were hugging each other with a love that only Jesus could bring about. Like myself, he is now part of the King's Church family at Aldershot, along with other policemen. We have in our church several members of the Surrey Police Christian Fellowship, of which I am also a member. Jesus will take two negatives and make them a positive. He can do what the world would look on as impossible and nonsense, so that all who witness it can see a superhuman power at work.

Police officers can become very sceptical because of their job. They witness so many of the evils that one human being can do to another. They witness some sickening things and they can become very bitter, suspicious and untrusting towards others. No wonder many of them take the problems of their job home with them, and their families suffer as a result. A police officer's life isn't an easy one, what with the stress of the work itself coupled with the sneers and jeers from much of the public, the pointing of fingers and being called names. I honestly don't know how some of them keep going, especially the Christian ones. But thank God they do. This country of ours would be chaos without our police force. On the whole they are a great bunch of men and women. You will always get the odd one who isn't, but they usually don't stay in the job long. I know of many Christian police officers who witness to criminals when they are brought in and placed in the cells. I know of many ex-criminals who have come to know Jesus through such an experience. And many Christian police, when they have to go to a home to break some bad news, will pray and share Jesus with the family, if the appropriate opportunity arises.

The highlight of my association with the Surrey Police Christian Fellowship was when the members decided to organise a meeting at their headquarters at Bourne House and invite many of their unsaved colleagues, including the Assistant Chief Constable. The evening would start off with a dinner and then I was to be the guest speaker. What a privilege, what an honour, what an opportunity to show these police officers what Jesus can do in an old villain's life!

I arrived at the Surrey Police Headquarters with Maureen and was met by some Police Christian Fellowship friends. Then Maureen and I were given a conducted tour. There were boards displaying crime rate statistics and so on. To think at one time I had been one of those statistics! But here I was being treated like royalty by the men I used to hate. Eventually, we sat down to our meal and I was placed next to the Assistant Chief Constable. We were talking to each other as if we had been lifelong pals and addressing each other by our first names, although he isn't a committed Christian. Here was a top policeman treating me with respect, as an equal. I had tears in my eyes. Only Jesus could have done this. I looked over to my old friend, traffic patrol man, Ted Stevens, and I saw that he was choked up and near to tears. He too could see the miracle of it all.

Then came the time to share my testimony with the police officers. I saw that they were dumbfounded with what they heard, and at the end, two policemen gave their lives to Jesus and many others were greatly moved.

It was an evening I will never forget. Since that time, either through church meetings, Full Gospel Business Men's Fellowship International dinners and other meetings, I have seen many police officers of all ranks come to the Lord. It makes nonsense of what the world would think, but my God is a God of the impossible.

4. *Prince of the Air*

The green flicker of the screen dominated our front room as I sat idly watching a recorded television programme. As I snapped off the remote control switch of the video playback machine, my mind wandered back to all those wasted years when I had spent so much time in front of the television screen. Television and video recordings had played such a large part in my old life. I could not begin to recall the number of hours I had spent watching "blue" movies, allowing them to sap my moral fibre until I was reduced to a ruthless monster, using sexual exploitation to gain easy money.

It began with what is known as "soft" pornography in my early days. But in reality there is no qualitative difference between "soft porn" and the hard stuff. Soft porn is motivated by the same unhealthy exploitation of basic human drives as that which leads to hardcore pornography. All sexual perversion is like a drug. As surely as soft drugs start their users off on the long and tortured trail to mainline addiction, so pornography grips the hearts of those who indulge. Recent scandals among evangelical Christian leaders in America prove the point. Unless the strings of Satan's domination of our lives are completely cut, he will always be able to manipulate us through a distortion of wholesome basic desires.

I was soon hooked on watching extreme pornography, and eventually I developed the connections to become a distributor of pornographic videos along the south coast. I quickly discovered that there was a fortune to be made through the apparently insatiable demand for the materials I was supplying.

My lifestyle became completely debauched. Promotion parties involving free sex led me to the point where my natural desires became dulled through overstimulation. Just as with drugs, it took more and more extreme forms to achieve the desired effect.

As I sat in the darkened front room I reflected that it was a miracle that I could now watch an ordinary programme with a clean mind. It wasn't always that way. When I first became a Christian, past associations tainted my thinking about television and video and I could not approach the media without a shudder of horror. It took the constant renewing of my mind by an act of the will and the work of the Holy Spirit to purify my approach to television in particular.

I knew that, from the moment of conversion, I was cleansed through the blood of Christ, completely forgiven and accepted by the Father as his son. Nevertheless, at another level, there was a constant battle to free myself from the shame of my past. Satan knows how to wrap his coils around the hearts and minds of his victims. Even after we are set free, his tentacles reach out to draw us back. Praise God, Jesus lovingly and patiently ministers to the willing soul through the influence of his Holy Spirit. Tenderly and gently he clears away the taint of the past which can so easily dominate our thinking. No wonder the apostle Paul exhorts us to wear the helmet of salvation. Satan knows where to attack and the mind is the last battleground he will ever relinquish.

As I sat into the evening, thinking about the powerful media which had so nearly wrecked our lives, I wondered what potential these same media had for good and for the Kingdom of God. The power of pornography had destroyed my marriage, reduced my wife to a zombie-like existence and shattered my relationship with my sons. Could not God use television and radio to produce the opposite effects?

I had often wondered what Paul meant when he described Satan as the "prince of the power of the air" (Eph. 2.2). Now I think I know. The air, or the atmosphere, is the medium through which we achieve ninety per cent of our communication. Whether it is by sight or sound, most of our sense impressions reach us through the air. What Paul is saying, when he gives our adversary the title of prince of the power of the air, is that he controls the main medium of communication. Ever since he tempted Eve's senses by whispering in her ear, "Has God said?" and by holding the luscious fruit before her, he has been busy corrupting every means of communication.

This is clearly illustrated by the emergence of the booming video industry in this country. Great Britain is proportionally the largest consumer of video film in the world, and we have the highest level of ownership of video machines. Britain has become the international video capital.

As soon as video took hold of the public imagination, Satan took control of it. Video is one of the most potent satanic tools at work in society. In itself it is neutral. It can be used for good or bad, but Satan seems to have cornered the market. The Church failed to see or to seize the opportunity video presented, so commercialism got in first. The industry is not uniformly bad, but it has its sharks and they tend to dominate. Quickly discerning that people would watch in private what they would never admit to viewing in public, the fly boys moved in. I know; I was one of them.

From my own experience, I can testify that it isn't just the riff-raff and the people at the bottom of society's pile who indulge in watching vicious and debauched videos. I have supplied politicians, judges, high-ranking police officers and other "respectable" citizens with pornographic material. Satan reaches into all levels of society by this means, to uneducated people, to public school pupils and to university graduates.

I am amazed at the depths of depravity reached in films readily available over the counter in home-video libraries and outlets, not to mention the under-the-counter stuff. At an even lower level is the kind of material I dealt with, which is not usually available even under the counter. This is circulated by rings dominated by the underworld. By these means the basest members of the underworld mix cheek by jowl with respectable society. The one gives credence and support to the other. In some cases I have known circulators of pornography to be sentenced by the very people who were their clients. In this way the moral fibre of the nation is being sapped by hypocrisy as well as sexual evil. Truly Satan is prince of the power of the air.

In the one area of the world where Christians have taken hold of the media to reach the public, Satan has also managed to work havoc. The aural and visual media are such powerful forces for generating wealth as well as for informing the mind and stimulating the imagination. Consequently, they have immense power to corrupt all who are involved in them. By their very nature they raise effective communicators to "star" status, and these celebrities can appear to become above criticism and so become corrupted by the media they attempt to exploit. In the process, their message inevitably becomes down-graded. Each fresh revelation of television evangelists who have been corrupted by power serves to shut off people to the message they preach. Recent sex scandals among Christian leaders in this arena in America are Satan's latest subtle strategy to distort the means of communication.

My own involvement in broadcasting has developed in a different way. Thank God it is still possible to appear on radio and television in this country simply to share your story.

As I mentioned in Chapter 2, my first experience of broadcasting took place when I was sharing the week of outreach meetings with Derek Brown and Trevor and Shirley Martin at the Kingsthorpe Christian Fellowship in Northampton. Lewis Houston felt that a good way of publicising the meetings would be to have me interviewed on local radio. Since I had such a colourful testimony he felt it would be a useful way of drawing attention to the meetings.

Lewis accompanied me to the BBC Radio Northampton studios. I was very apprehensive, not knowing what to expect since I had never set foot in a radio station before. As we sat in the reception area I was so nervous that we realised that the only thing to do was to take the matter to the Lord. So Lewis and I prayed together, lifting all my worries up to the Lord. The studio personnel must have wondered what was going on!

I said to Lewis, "If this is the Lord's will, then he will give the interviewer the right questions that I can answer, and he will give me the wisdom to answer the questions he asks me." I believed God was saying to me, "Ron, don't preach the Bible to them, but rather introduce them to the one who wrote it!"

The presenter who interviewed me turned out to be tremendously reassuring. Although he asked me some ambiguous questions and some that were pretty embarrassing, we were able to do an impressive recording in which the Lord got all the glory. It was a great time. Afterwards, the interviewer and many of the studio people said how heartened they were by what they heard.

Months later, I was to hear that a man driving up the M1 motorway switched on to Radio Northampton and, hearing my testimony, gave his life to the Lord then and there. Such is the power of Jesus.

Subsequently, I have broadcast often on local radio and on television. It has become almost a standard routine of longer outreach missions for the organisers to arrange for me to be interviewed on local radio at the beginning of the mission. I have been pleasantly surprised to find how open local radio presenters are to doing these interviews. Many of these local stations cover potential audiences of two to three million people. Among the stations which have broadcast my testimony are Two Counties Radio in Dorset, Radio Mercury, Radio Sheffield, Radio Essex and Red Dragon Radio in Cardiff as well as BBC Cardiff. Radio Essex was a high spot as I was interviewed with soccer star Glen Hoddle who testified clearly to the powerful work of Jesus in his life.

My first opportunity for television broadcasting arose out of a tent campaign in which we were involved at Bewdley in the West Midlands. More about that remarkable week will be described later, but suffice it to say for now that the campaign spilled over onto the streets. We even preached in two public houses. The landlords treated it as a bit of a joke, but if we wanted to go in and share the gospel that was all right with them. Even in the pubs we were seeing souls won, people giving their hearts to the Lord Jesus. In one particular pub where I talked to a number of people, the landlord had actually advertised that I would be there. Together we spread the gospel and I shared my testimony with between thirty and forty customers in an upper room of the pub. It was a no-holds-barred session and became very lively.

At the end, an attractive young woman came up to me and introduced herself. She turned out to be a researcher for Central Television, working for a programme called *The Michael Hart Contact*. She told me that she had never witnessed anything like this before and asked whether I would like to appear with my wife on Central Television within a couple of weeks. I agreed instantly.

About a fortnight after the Bewdley Tent Mission we went up to Central Television at the invitation of Michael Hart, the producer of the *Contact* television show, which goes out every Wednesday lunchtime throughout the Midlands area.

We were put up overnight in a five-star hotel and Maureen found it difficult to come to terms with this. I had been used to this kind of luxury in my old way of life, but Maureen hadn't. Early the next morning we were whisked off to the Central Television studios where we saw a number of famous people, and were introduced to Michael Hart. It was then that we discovered that Michael is a Spirit-filled Christian. He is a man really sold out for God. So much so, that it probably cost him his job as producer of the well-known television soap opera *Crossroads*.

Before the show went on, we were shown around the studios. Michael talked to us before we went on. "Do you realise the average church congregation is fifty people?" he asked. Then he went on to say, "If you preached for thirty years, seven days a week to the average-sized church, that is approximately the size of your audience today." This did nothing to help the state of my nerves. My stomach muscles tightened up and I began to sweat profusely. At last I said, "Well, Lord, here is the chance. We have the opportunity to preach to several million."

We were eventually led through to the operational studio. Lights flashed, the countdown began, and Maureen and I were appearing live on the programme. We were able to share our testimonies, our story and the love of Jesus. I explained how if anyone is in Christ Jesus they become a new creation, old things have passed away, and all things are new.

I do not know how many, of the thousands who heard our story that day, came to a realisation of who Jesus is. I honestly believe that we will never fully know the impact of that sowing. What really amazed us was that after the programme we came and sat down in the back room of the studios and Michael Hart came in with the production team. We stood up and Michael prayed to the Lord, offering the whole programme up to Jesus. I never thought I would ever see this, a top producer for a television show praying in the Spirit in his own work environment. There were people there who were religious, people who didn't believe in the Lord, but there were also born-again, Spirit-filled people, like Michael, Maureen and myself, offering up the programme to God. I could really see that the Lord was into television as well as radio. God has his people strategically located in the media and I believe that eventually – when his time is right – many more programmes dealing with real spiritual issues and presenting the claims of the Lord will emerge in Britain.

Our experience of television wasn't to end with the Jonathan Hart programme. In October 1987, Maureen and I took part in a chat show called *The Once A Week Show* for CVG Television, a cable television company based in Crawley. I was interviewed for about seven minutes, and this was such a success, praise God, that the director and producers felt they should produce a short feature film of my life story.

Arrangements were set up to begin shooting on Wednesday, 4th November. What a day that was! The film crew arrived at our house at 9.30 a.m. and after much moving around of furniture, the lighting and sound equipment was set up. We filmed in the house for about three hours and after lunch continued filming out of doors with Maureen and me walking round the estate. As you can imagine, this raised a few eyebrows, but yet again it gave us a great opportunity to witness. We then carried on to the village where shots were taken near the green and around the shopping precinct.

The director felt it would be good to shoot some more film on location in some of my old haunts. He asked me to seek advice from the governor of Rochdale Prison as they wanted to film sequences related to my life in prison. Subsequently, we filmed there as well as in my home town of Basingstoke, and in and around the village knocking on doors. We were also able to get some footage with my old friend Trefor Jones, who was minister at the local Baptist church in Hartley Wintney when we first became Christians.

The project is now complete and is available in video cassette form. My prayer is that it will reach thousands or even millions of people, not only through CVG and Church Cinema Presentations, but also by being screened on our major television channels.

It is time for God to show who is really the prince of the air. Communication was the first area of human experience which Satan corrupted. I believe God is in the business of wresting back from Satan's grasp everything that he has ever falsely claimed from God through human weakness and sin. It is God's desire to open channels of communication with us. He did it most graphically and starkly by sending his Son, Jesus Christ, in the flesh to be a man among us. Some Christians want nothing to do with radio and television or television evangelism, but I think that the presentation of truth through visual and aural means is right in line with what the Father was doing by sending Jesus into the world. Jesus was described as the Word of God. As long as we never abandon the Word and his essential message, every one of the communications media is a valid means of bringing God's message to the attention of lost men and women.

Recent events in the realm of television evangelism do not invalidate this claim at all. They merely demonstrate that Satan is so rattled when Christians capture the media that he will tempt them, oppose them and do anything he can to invalidate their efforts. He knows that effective Christian communication can be a danger to his kingdom.

Of course, whatever medium of communication we use, we have to remember never to distort the message in favour of the means. We also have to grasp the fact that, in the end, whatever the channels we use to get the message across, it is the Holy Spirit who convicts men and women of sin and brings them home to the Saviour. Any attempt on our parts to use a powerful tool like television or radio to coerce or manipulate is to fall into Satan's pattern of thinking. Those are tactics which he uses and which Christians should never, ever employ. After all, "the weapons of our warfare are not carnal but mighty through God to the pulling down of strongholds; casting down imaginations and every high thing that exalts itself against the knowledge of God, and bringing into captivity every thought to the obedience of Christ" (2 Cor. 10. 4–5).

Manipulation is Satan's game. Those are the tactics I was caught up in when I dealt in pornography. Having used the media in my foolishness to corrupt, defile and ruin many people when I was a tool of Satan, I now want to use them to exalt my Saviour. He is the Prince of Peace and as such he is entitled to take to himself the designation "Prince of the power of the air". Satan is a pretender who will one day be dethroned, and I believe that the media will have a part to play, one way or another, in preparing the world for the final showdown.

5. Christ in the Classroom

The roots of my criminal career were planted in my childhood. Cursed and battered by my mother and largely ignored by my father, I saw the adult world as hostile and alien. No wonder that by the time I reached school I was already opposed to authority. Satan had set me up so that I was unable to benefit from education. My attitude was aggressive and unreasoning; I hit out at the system around me and consequently benefited little from it. I am glad that today I am able to redress the balance to some extent as I visit schools and colleges throughout the country.

Young people today get a bad press. They are branded as irresponsible, feckless, and anti-authority. Much of the adult world stereotypes young people as noisy, rebellious and foul-mouthed drug takers who then find strange and threatening. It is true that many of them live in a youth culture which is bewildering to the average adult. Yet it is this same adult generation which helps to create and certainly exploits this culture to its own financial advantage.

Many youngster are simply people who have lost their way. Often they see no hope for life and no future for the world. Unemployment faces many of them and they find it difficult to make sense of conflicting adult values in a society threatened by the spectre of nuclear warfare.

But it is we Christians who have let this generation down most of all. We don't practise on Monday what we preach in our churches on Sunday. Some of the country's top church leaders deny the truth of the Bible. Many of them will take out this from the Bible and put in that; accept one bit and reject another. Even conservative evangelical Christians play the same game when they say one part of the Bible is for today while another isn't. In so doing, they water down the gospel until it has no power.

Power for living is to be found in the essential gospel message of the whole Bible. If you leave some bits out or downgrade others, it is like tripping the circuit breaker that prevents the power getting through. The apostle Paul said, "I am not ashamed of the gospel for it is the power of God for salvation to everyone who believes" (Rom. 1.16).

Young people today are not fools: they can see the hypocrisy of Bible-denying Christians. I am so glad that now I can go into the schools and preach the real gospel, the message of hope, and see so many of the pupils respond as do the prisoners in the prisons. They are ready to believe in Jesus Christ. When confronted, they accept what he did and said, and they are ready to give their lives to him.

The stumbling block comes when you mention the word "church". To young people it is identified with dullness, irrelevance and unreality. I praise God, however, that many of our churches of all denominations are changing, some faster than others, so that in almost every school to which I go I can pass young converts on to a live and real experience of church life.

Over the past three or four years it has been my privilege to preach and teach in both state and independent schools throughout the country. Often I am not only allowed in to take morning assemblies, but I am also invited to speak in the classrooms and to visit school Christian Unions. Some of these have been memorable visits.

My work in schools began in local state schools where I would be asked to speak at assemblies. Over a period, such a rapport has grown up with some of the schools that I have been asked to speak in religious education lessons over an extended period throughout a school. I have been very much blessed by ministering in some local secondary schools, for the feedback I have received from teachers indicates that the seeds planted go on growing. Not only the youngsters are touched by hearing the gospel message, but God's word can spread to teachers and parents too.

I have also been privileged to speak in some of the nation's top public schools including Wellington College, Marlborough and Charterhouse. Our two visits to Charterhouse School were memorable. A total of forty-five pupils made a commitment to Christ and there is now a thriving Christian group there, whereas there was previously only a handful of students in the Christian Union. The people from our top schools today will become tomorrow's politicians, lawyers, judges and leaders. Remember, John Wesley was educated at Charterhouse. We need to take the Christian message to the people at the top as well as those at the bottom. Together we can change the face of the country for Christ.

When we first went to Charterhouse I didn't know what to expect. I knew that I didn't speak correct English and I was concerned that because of this, and my obvious lack of education, my message would not be well received. However, I found the pupils attentive and courteous, and when I made an appeal for them to commit their lives to Christ, thirty-five responded.

Thank God for Christian members of staff who were willing to follow up and consolidate the results of this visit. Subsequently, two of the teachers set up weekly Bible study groups so that those who were interested could learn more about the Christian faith in an informal atmosphere of fellowship and mutual encouragement.

One Sunday in June 1987 a miracle took place at Marlborough College in Wiltshire. The invitation to talk at the school had come from the school chaplain via a mutual acquaintance. The chaplain was a great warrior for Jesus, but not many of the pupils or other staff were born-again believers. How tragic this is when you realise that this college, along with many other public schools, was built on Christian foundations.

The first miracle was that I was allowed into this place at all. There had been objections to the invitation being issued to me, and it was only the day before that the staff had relented and withdrawn their objections to my coming. Now they were even prepared to use my meeting as an alternative to their usual Sunday service.

After a meal, we were taken to a hall which held about 200 people, including the headmaster and his wife, the staff and a large number of the students. I preached on the power of Jesus in these days and how privileged they were to be thought of as the cream of society. I told them they would be the future doctors, barristers and politicians: people who would be in the top echelons of society, guiding this country. I pointed out to them with a boldness granted by the Holy Spirit that if they didn't believe in Jesus and weren't born again or committed to Christian morals, there was little chance for the rest of the country. I then shared my story with them.

As I finished, I asked them to bow their heads and we would pray for God's Spirit to visit us in power and truth. Nervously, I took a sip of water and prayed under my breath: "Dear Lord, this old fellow [meaning the chaplain] has stuck to his guns for you. Please save half a dozen souls, just to encourage him because he really loves you." I then said a public prayer and gave an invitation for those present to repent and give their hearts to Jesus. Again, under my breath, I was saying, "Come on, Jesus, give us at least half a dozen."

I underestimated the power of God. When I opened my eyes I was amazed at the number who had stood up to commit their hearts to Jesus. It must have been at least forty people, including some members of staff. Now the questions many doubting Christians will ask are: "Will they keep going?" or "Will it last?" I never doubt that when God reaps a harvest he is quite capable of turning that grain into living bread. I know that Jesus is Lord and that he is sovereign over this and every situation.

Another memorable visit for us was when I was invited to speak at the Royal Agricultural College at Cirencester in Gloucestershire. This engagement was to lead to a chain of remarkable events.

The meeting took place on a Tuesday evening in June. Maureen and I arrived in time to be entertained to an evening meal in the college dining hall before going on to take the meeting. I preached my heart out, but at the meeting only one person responded to the invitation to ask Christ to come into their lives.

I was a little disappointed at the response, but I learned later that many were touched and within the next few days two young men had made commitments. The person who had responded at the meeting was a nineteen-year-old girl who was visiting a Christian friend at the college. She was in deep trouble, having become involved with a married man who had children nearly her age. She was now pregnant by him, he could not marry her, and her parents were threatening to disown her if she did not have an abortion.

This girl wrote to me later to tell me that she was reconciled with God and was also hoping for a reconciliation with her parents. She was sure that her coming to the college and hearing me preach was a direct result of God's intervention. It had looked as though circumstances would prevent her from visiting her friend at Cirencester, but at the last minute she had felt how important it was for her to get there and then everything had worked out so that she was able to get to the college just in time for the meeting.

As I have said, when you touch young people you are often also reaching out to their families through them. About a month after the visit to Cirencester I was booked to preach at a meeting held in a theatre on the seafront at Swanage. When I entered the theatre I was handed a letter, and before I stood up to preach I felt the Lord prompting me to read it. It was from the brother of a Christian Union student at Cirencester. He had heard about my visit to the college and his brother had lent him my book. Now he was writing to me for prayer for his father who was in Southampton Hospital. In two days' time he was due to have a very tricky operation to remove a blockage of his spinal cord.

After I had given my message that night many people gave their lives to the Lord and many were healed. I then asked the people present to join me in prayer for the father of the man who had written to me.

Two or three weeks later I had a letter from the wife of the sick man. She told me that at the very moment I had prayed publicly for her husband, he had heard a crack in his back and had felt movement returning to his legs. When the surgeon saw him the next day he was baffled, but agreed that the operation was now unnecessary. He had been discharged from hospital and, while not yet completely healed, was walking again and enjoying a holiday in Wales.

Touch youngsters in the classroom and you will touch their families at home. The message I preach to the young people is often as relevant to their parents.

Many parents condemn young people today for their drug taking, recklessness and promiscuity. They are right to be concerned. We know that drugs maim and kill and that they are related to many other evils. But many of these same parents smoke cigarettes without realising that they are addictive as well as being a much more significant cause of illness and death than illegal drugs.

Many older people are hypocrites and people of double standards. Middle-aged people condemn the youth of today because of their promiscuity, but much of today's moral laxity began in our youth in the 1960s. The evils which so many of our young people are reaping today are what were sown in the past by their parents' generation. But, I praise Jesus, the young people of today, as never before, are looking for an answer, seeking for something more. We have that answer and I have been privileged to take Christ into the classroom, bringing the message of Jesus to young people up and down the country. It is a message of hope and I am glad that so many are willing to respond. If I had been given the opportunity to hear about Christ when I was still at school, I might never have wasted so many years. Save a young person and you save not only a soul, but a life for Jesus.

6. Children of the Kingdom

Most convicts, however tough, have a soft spot for children. Nobody is more despised or badly treated by the other inmates in a prison than the child abuser. Frequently, such offenders have to be kept in solitary confinement to protect them from the other prisoners.

Maybe this regard for children has something to do with a lost or deprived childhood. A high proportion of prisoners suffered cruelty or neglect from parents. Once confined, a criminal's mind seems to focus on these things. With some, the concern is merely sentimental – heaven knows, many of them have neglected or deserted their own children. Certainly they gave little thought to them when engaging in the criminal activity which led to a jail sentence.

All the same, many criminals have a genuine love for children. I know that I do, and the events of my tragic first marriage and my criminal activities at that time were partly motivated by a desire to keep the family together. My first wife would leave me whenever I wasn't running around with other crooks, bringing in the rewards of a vicious life. The loss of my first family and the painful experience of building up another one has left me with a love for little ones, and some of this has rubbed off on my ministry. Some of the most remarkable healings I have seen have centred around children.

I have already mentioned my first visit to Roger Lockwood's church in Wellingborough, on the occasion when I made my first attempt to preach in a prison. After the morning service we went home and had lunch with Roger and his wife. Then I went to lie down because I was pretty exhausted. I had been up since the early hours of the morning and the experience of what had happened in the prison had drained me physically and emotionally. I had only been lying down on the bed for a couple of minutes when the telephone rang and Roger came up to my bedroom and said, "Ron, I have had a telephone call from a couple whose son is in hospital. He has met with a pretty serious accident to his eye and they would like us to go in and pray for him. They have heard about you and they would like you to pray for his eye."

Apparently Toby had been playing in the woods with some of his friends and he had staked his eye with a piece of wood which had penetrated the eyeball. There had been inflammation in the back of the eye and the hospital had to operate to relieve the pressure caused by fluid at the back of the eye. It looked as though he was going to lose the sight of that eye. I somewhat reluctantly went with Roger. It is one thing praying for elderly people, but when a young boy really believes that if you pray for him he is going to receive his sight, this tests your faith to the limits.

Roger and I went to the hospital where we spent quite a long time outside praying in tongues to the Lord. I was trying to summon a faith which I felt I just didn't have. In the end we decided we had better go in, as it was getting late and visiting hours were almost over. We started to walk down the corridor towards the ward when we were stopped by the sister there who asked us who we were. In fact she asked me if I was the CID. I laughed and said that nothing could be further from the truth. I explained who I was, and what we were there for, and she let us go into the room where Toby was lying on the bed with a big patch over his eye.

I said to the Lord, "It is not such a bad deal for somebody to lose one eye. At least he has got one good eye, he is not blind, he will be able to see." But Toby really believed that the Lord was going to heal him if I prayed for him. He threw his arms around me and started to cry and I hugged him and cried with him. I was praying, "Please give me faith," for at that moment I had none. Then the Lord gave me a vision and he spoke to me in my spirit and said, "Do you remember the time when I healed the blind man and my disciples said to me, 'Why was he blind in the first place? Was it the sin that he had committed or his parents?' I said, 'Neither. He was blind that I may heal him to glorify my Father who is in heaven.'" The Lord said, "This boy will be healed to glorify me in this hospital."

I prayed with that lad and I knew beyond any doubt that the Lord was going to touch him and that his eye would be made well. After I had prayed with him I spoke to his parents. I called them outside and told them, "Although you may not believe, never let your son see your unbelief. Let him believe and go on encouraging him." Roger assured me that he would continue to visit Toby and pray and see this through to the end.

As we left the hospital I said to Roger, "I know that boy is going to receive his sight. I know the miracle has happened." Roger looked at me and smiled and said, "Yes, I know too; praise God."

A couple of weeks later I received a letter from Roger in which he told me that Toby and his father were in church on Sunday morning and both of them had testified to the healing of the Lord in Toby's eye. His eyesight was now virtually healed and he was able to read Psalm 91 which the Lord had given him as a promise when he was in hospital.

*

At a three-day mission in South Wales which I shared with Richard Whitehouse and some members of his church from Hounslow, two children were ministered to in a remarkable way. Neither is completely healed yet, but in that mission God began something special in each of their lives.

The first was Gareth, a young boy of about seven years of age who sat at the front with his parents at one of our meetings. He was severely brain damaged and unable to walk, as the result of a swimming accident some months previously. Richard had preached from John chapter 5 on the man at the pool of Bethesda. He based his message around the question of Jesus to the paralysed man, "Do you really want to be made whole?" At the end Richard said, "I know there is someone here who is not sure that they want to see their healing."

Gareth's father broke down in tears as he stood and acknowledged that when he was asked to bring his son to the meeting he had struggled with God about it. He was unemployed and felt that the family could not manage without the boy's disability allowance. As he wrestled with this problem he cried out, "Jesus, I want Gareth to get well." Maureen and I went to pray with the boy, and as I moved towards him, under the inspiration of the Holy Spirit I reached out my hand and said, "Come on, Gareth, let's go home." He instantly got up out of his wheelchair and walked across the room to meet me. We then walked around together.

He became very agitated when his parents wanted to put him back in the chair. The paralysis was gone, but the brain damage had not. Prior to this Gareth was aggressive and snarled when strangers approached him. Ever since he has been docile and affectionate. When approached, he will put his arms around your neck and say, "Pray, pray." Much to the embarrassment of his humanistic and unbelieving doctor, when he visits the home Gareth insists on being prayed for!

A couple of years later Gareth is making progress. Recently, for the first time in his life, he picked up the telephone, dialled the correct number and spoke to the person at the other end! I believe God will complete the work he has begun.

The mission in Dinas Powis in South Wales was organised during the church holiday which Maureen and I had been invited to share with Richard Whitehouse's fellowship from Hounslow. We became close to many of the fellowship, including Laurence and Paula Brown. Paula led the musicians for the evening outreach meetings in the scout hut. As I got to know the family, I found myself increasingly drawn to Laurence and Paula's three-year-old daughter, Amy.

Amy was a hemiplegic: the right side of her body was paralysed. She was also almost completely deaf in one ear and partially deaf in the other. She used to ride about on a little plastic tricycle. Although she was so severely handicapped, she was a lovely sunny child and I felt sure that the Lord was planning to do something special in her life.

During one of the outreach meetings, we were praying for the sick and suddenly Amy came scooting up the aisle on her little tricycle as though she, too, was coming forward for prayer. I really didn't know what to think. I was afraid of being carried away by my affection for the child and my desire to see God working in her life; how could I be sure that she really had come for healing? But as I looked down at Amy I felt that the Lord was reassuring me that she had, indeed, come out to be prayed for. I asked the Lord, "Surely she doesn't know what we are doing?" and he replied, "No, but I do." So I took her in my arms and, with Laurence and Paula and Richard and Margaret Whitehouse, prayed for Amy's healing. I prophesied that by the time she was ten, Amy's healing would be complete.

I have faith that the Lord will honour that prophecy and so do Amy's parents. From that day Amy's condition has improved considerably. She has grown, gained weight, is straighter and has started to walk. She is still partially deaf, but has now started to communicate in recognisable words and phrases. What is more, she has a sparkle about her that people cannot help noticing. Jesus is working in her and it shows.

Laurence and Paula's faith was built up so much by what the Lord was doing for Amy that they felt able to uproot themselves and join Richard and Margaret who had been called to live and minister in Wales. They were so sure that this was what the Lord wanted that they did not ascertain beforehand what facilities there would be for Amy. In fact the facilities turned out to be far better than in Middlesex. Many of the professionals dealing with Amy are Christians, and they have responded very positively to the family's assurance of Amy's eventual healing. Amy has started school and has been able to join a school for normal children which has a special needs unit. Many people have been touched by this little girl and by her parents' faith, and the Lord has spoken to others independently of how he will complete what he has started for Amy.

You see, God not only heals the children, he works through them. Each of the cases I have cited are of children from Christian homes. Christians are not exempt from trouble and it is particularly distressing when it affects our children. Sometimes we wish we could suffer for them. But there is a better way than that. The word of God makes it clear that the children of believing parents are sanctified. That does not mean they are saved by their parents' faith, because none of us can be redeemed through the faith of another. However, it does mean that such children have a special relationship with God. Through the parents, God has a special channel of communication to touch the lives of these children.

It is a privilege and a tremendous responsibility to be a Christian parent. Whether your children are ill or healthy, you are the means of making God real to them. Through your faith it is possible to show your children what God can do. I cannot help wishing that I had been brought up in a Christian home instead of being abused and battered as a child. What God did in my life proves that the Lord Jesus cares about all children. But the children of Christian parents are special. They are children of the Kingdom.

7. *Tabernacles in the Wilderness*

During the early part of 1986 I began studying the life of Moses. As a character he impressed me because of the energy of his nature, his leadership abilities and, most of all, his walk with God. I was struck by how, in spite of his privileged upbringing in the palaces of Pharaoh, Moses never forgot his origins. Indeed, it was his fierce loyalty to his own people which caused him to sin by committing the murder which led to him becoming a criminal on the run. I had a certain fellow feeling for Moses.

I was intrigued by the way in which, once he had met the Lord for himself, Moses was led by God in the wilderness by means of the pillar of cloud by day and the pillar of fire by night. The account of how God told him to build the tabernacle gripped me. Here were God's people worshipping in a tent in the wilderness.

As I reflected, it was as though the Lord specifically said, "People won't come to church, so you take the church to the people." I began to picture tents on village greens all over the country and people coming into those tents to hear the word of the Lord, just as children would go to a circus.

I shared this idea with a number of people. I was so young in the Lord then that I imagined I was the first person ever to think of using tents to preach the gospel in this country. I now began to learn that it had been done before and I have since read several books on the subject. There didn't seem any way, however, that the finances and all the necessary organisation could come together for me to be involved in tent crusade work. Nevertheless, one Sunday morning in our church I was introduced to a minister by the name of George Muller. He was an Elim pastor who had just come back from South Africa where he had been ministering. We chatted for a while and I was amazed when he started to tell me of a vision he had to bring a tent mission to the little town of Bewdley in Worcestershire. He said that he had received this vision while attending Reinhard Bonnke's meetings in South Africa. One of George's friends, Oliver Raper, is the United Kingdom representative for Bonnke's organisation "Christ For All Nations", and he also shared this vision of tent missions.

As we shared our complementary visions, George said, "Well, keep praying, Ron. We believe that this tent mission is right and in view of what you are saying I believe you should be part of it. We have no money, we don't know where the finance is coming from, but we are believing God for it."

I went home impressed by this apparently chance conversation, but I have long since learned that God does nothing by chance. So I meditated and prayed, coming to believe that George and Oliver's vision would be realised and I would have a part to play in it. In the next few weeks I received a telephone call from George, who told me that the Riverside Rowing Club at Bewdley had offered a plot of ground, a grass field, and offered to supply the electricity for lighting. They had also received an offer of a 500-seater tent at about half the normal price. They were going to run the tent mission from 7th–13th July, 1986. George asked me and Maureen to be part of this, together with Oliver Raper and Noel Shepherd. We were going to have a tremendous time. We were believing great things for the Lord. What was more significant, every church in and around the Bewdley area was going to be involved; every church gave it its full backing.

On the first night there was a tremendous response. We had 400 people there. The offering that night almost covered the expense of the tent, so we were really looking forward to great things. We saw startling events happen that week. Besides the tent mission we were also having open air meetings in the street; we were going into pubs and clubs and everywhere we could possibly spread the gospel. Every night the meetings grew bigger and bigger. The second night there were 600 people present and the third saw 800. Many, many people every night were getting saved; dozens of people were coming out making decisions for the Lord Jesus. Many bodies were being healed, delivered and set free. It was like Bible days. I have never seen anything like it before. It was just as if Jesus was walking in our midst. We were seeing massive signs and wonders and many conversions.

I remember one particular Wednesday afternoon meeting I took specifically for the unemployed. There is a lot of unemployment in the area and I wanted to share with people that Jesus loved them even though they were unemployed, and that the Lord had plenty of vacancies for evangelists. There were millions of people in the world and in our country who needed to be saved. At the end I gave an altar call. There weren't many people there, but all of a sudden a great big fellow stood up and came forward and started to break down. He said he wanted his life cleaned up and he wanted to give his heart to Jesus. He was an alcoholic. As George and I prayed for him he fell down under the Holy Spirit's power. When he got up he said, "I know I have been delivered from alcoholism." He came to the meetings every night and returned on the last night to testify that he hadn't drunk for four days. On the Friday, when he went down to pick up his Giro cheque (which he normally drew out only to spend in the nearest pub), he had returned home and given it all to his wife to buy food and to pay the rent. This was something he had not been able to do for many, many years.

There were deaf people who were healed and could hear. One man had suffered two strokes, but he stood up out of his wheelchair and was healed. That is how things continued. There is no way that I could tell you all the things that happened that week. What I can tell you is that the crowds grew to the extent that on the last night we had to take the sides of the 500-seater tent down. There must have been around 1,000 people, something that had never been witnessed in the whole history of that little village of Bewdley. Our records show that during the course of the week over 270 decisions were made for Jesus at the tent meetings. That is not counting the people who were saved in the street and in the pubs and in the coffee bars and women's meetings. We are still waiting to learn the total number of people who were saved. Testimonies of healings are still coming in to me and to George and Oliver's office in Worcester.

I had learned there was something really special about tent missions. Maybe my enthusiasm is something to do with the fact that I come from travelling stock. Certainly there is something like the circus atmosphere, and just as you see people flocking to a circus, people seem so uninhibited about coming to a tent. There is something great about getting up there in a tent and sharing Jesus in the open air. It is marvellous. I believe that if a tent was good enough for Moses to travel with and for the Lord to make his abode with his people, there must be a lot going for tent missions. I knew that this was something new that was happening for me and in the future I was to take part in many tent missions and I hope that I will take part in many more to come. I do believe this is one of the many evangelistic arms of the real Church of God, the people who are really seeking the Lord in Spirit and in truth. If the public are not coming into the churches, we have got to take Jesus to them. And I believe that by taking a tent onto a village green or into a town or park and travelling around with the message, we are going to see a mighty harvest in this way won for Jesus.

The following year saw our involvement in another tent mission. Smaller than the first, it nevertheless had disproportionate effects on the neighbourhood. The event took place on a weekend in July in the small village of Crawley Down in Sussex. It came about as a result of the vision of two of the local leaders, Paul Taylor and Glynn Phillips, after they had visited my home to consult with me. Together with others they put in much prayer and preparation.

I cannot find words to describe my admiration for this small group of Christians; for their faith, commitment and love for Jesus. There is no way that I could put into words the things we saw, heard and did in the holy name of Jesus. Paul Taylor is endeavouring to write a full account of the building of the mission, the mission itself and its ongoing effects.

On entering the village we were amazed to see, on almost every telegraph post and on trees, prominently placed bright red posters advertising the mission, which was entitled "Aflame '87".

The meeting on Saturday was very well attended, but we knew that these numbers would increase as each day of the mission went on. Barry Stevens, a friend from a church in Frimley, near my home, was present. A number of his church members, including deacons, came down for the first evening meeting. And they, with many others, were not only blessed, but received the baptism of the Holy Spirit.

Over the three days we saw people saved and felt the power of God. I am sure this was the result of the nonstop prayer offered up to God by this small band of warriors of Jesus at Crawley Down. I have never experienced, seen or heard of any fellowship or church where its people have prayed so long and faithfully for revival. This little band started off only a few years ago from nothing and is rapidly growing, not only in numbers, not only in grace, but in the love of Jesus Christ.

Some remarkable events took place as a result of this mission, including a sustained attack from Satanists. I have reserved the details for a later chapter, but Fred Lemon and I had not witnessed such opposition before. I was glad we were working together. In the end Jesus received the glory, many were saved and healed, the fellowship there increased by sixty per cent and on the last night we had to take down the sides of the small tent as a crowd of maybe 150–200 gathered.

I don't believe that this will be our last taste of tent missions. It is one area of evangelism which I have a heart to develop in the future. The financial outlay is high, but when churches band together it is not prohibitive. Moreover, when churches work together in a tent mission, barriers between them seem to be broken down in a way which they aren't in a conventional church building. Tents are a reminder that we are a pilgrim people building tabernacles in the wilderness to the glory of our God.

8. A Hard Lesson

For eighteen months I had witnessed many miraculous things in my ministry. There were stories of outstanding conversions in and out of prisons. Many healings and miracles had taken place throughout the country and I was growing in boldness for the Lord. But the devil would never give up and he wasn't going to stop and sit around while I went about stealing his people and setting them free with the word of God.

I believe, like many of the front-line ministries, I was now one of Satan's special targets. As far as he was concerned I had to be stopped. Unwittingly, I helped him in his task. The first thing he needed to do to stop me was to move God's hedge of protection from around me, get me to let down my shield. We all have weaknesses and it is those that the adversary will work on. Every individual, every church, every ministry is only as strong as its weakest link. It is your weakest link that will cause you to break down. The devil knows where that weak link is, and that is the place where he will enter, in the hope of exploiting your weakness and destroying you.

Without me knowing it, the devil had been working on me for a long time. Against the advice of my leaders I had been taking on far too many commitments. I had been giving out too much and taking in too little. You can't motor round the world on one tank of petrol. You will have to call in at petrol stations at regular intervals to be topped up. It is so important for every Christian to be regularly topped up. We need to take in nurture to enable us to carry on.

Many people have asked me, "Do you have to go to church to be a Christian?" and my usual reply is, "Can you be an alcoholic without going to a public house or an off-licence?" But despite my theory that everyone needs to belong to a church, I was neglecting my own needs in that direction. I was not getting enough fellowship and worship for its own sake. Few people realise the amount of time in prayer and study that goes into working full-time for Jesus. The constant miles of travelling, taking meetings, then praying for people after them – often into the small hours of the morning – took more out of me than a twelve-hour day used to when I worked in motorway construction. Then there was the strain of being parted days on end from my family. Life was becoming more and more stressful.

I was at a physical and spiritual low by the end of October 1986. Derek Brown, my friend and leader of the church, called me to one side at a conference we were both attending. He told me in brotherly love, "Ron, you are treading on dangerous ground," and gave me a lot of other good advice. Derek went on to tell me that only a few days previously, while leaving a meeting with his wife, he had an overwhelming sense in his spirit that my life was in danger. The Lord had obviously used him to warn me, but I rejected his advice. This was later to prove almost fatal to me.

Besides being drained physically and spiritually, I was also being attacked verbally, and in letters, by some Christians. There seemed to be a lot of back stabbing and gossip. Actually it was only a tiny proportion of all the people I had come in contact with, but I was now down to a point where this very small minority became more significant than the majority. I was focusing in and listening to the negatives. It came to a point where the criticism was all I could hear. The devil had found my weak point and was about to destroy me if he could.

You see, my weak point was other Christians. I went into prisons and expected trouble and insults, but I didn't get them. I got respect. If I went into pubs, brothels, drug squats, street corners, I would be ready for trouble and abuse, but again I got respect. These people seemed to love me for the message of hope I was bringing them. I love my fellow brothers and sisters in Christ Jesus and I never expected to get opposition from that quarter. That is the downfall of many people's ministries. The breaking point in many of their lives is when the enemy attacks from within their own ranks.

I had made a very silly mistake. I had begun to look at the person instead of the sin. We are all sinners saved by grace and none of us will ever be perfect. I started to judge certain people and bitterness crept in. I was on a very slippery slope that would almost end in disaster, but I praise God that he can turn what seems like certain defeat into victory. And if he is going to take us from one degree of glory to another we have to be refined like gold. I needed to be refined before my ministry was going to move into another dimension for the Lord.

By the end of November, I had cancelled a lot of my appointments. I knew I wasn't right with the Lord. The Lord had to sort me out or the devil would destroy me. I had, as I said before, bitterness in my heart, and was judging people. Most of the trouble came through a very few people. They were mainly people who had had a good education and had been following God for years and had prayed and thought that they had a ministry. When they saw a jumped-up, uneducated ex-convict being used by the Lord, and the many doors that were being opened up for me, they resented it and were bitter and jealous. I guess some folks have never read 1 Corinthians chapter 1 verses 27–29. I should not have listened. I should have prayed for them, and then asked my leaders to pray for me to take away the hurt.

I was later to be shown by Jesus that it wasn't just hurt, but pride – yet another area of my life that needed sorting out. You see, the devil can use anyone to do his evil works; he even used Peter to denounce Jesus. We are just flesh. I hope that through this account, readers will learn to love the very people who hurt them, even those nearest and dearest to them. Remember, hate the sin but love the sinner.

By December I had decided to give up my ministry. I wasn't going to give up Jesus. I could never do that; I loved him so much and he meant so much to me. But I just wanted to be an ordinary Christian, to go to church, but have no more travelling, preaching and getting involved in other people's problems. I didn't need the hassle. I didn't get that when I was in the world.

What was happening to me was causing Maureen great concern. She had received a vision from the Lord that this was going to end with me having a heart attack. The Lord had saved me from certain death six years previously when I had suffered two massive heart attacks and actually died clinically. But what he then instructed me to do was to go out to the world to preach the gospel, heal the sick and drive out demons. Freely you have received, freely give: that was the condition I agreed to when Jesus raised me up from that death bed. I had accepted that he was going to send me out to be used, but now I was going back on the covenant we had made together. I no longer wanted to keep my part of the bargain. In consequence, although I was still a Christian, I was effectively banishing Jesus from my life. I was going

76

to do my own thing, not what he had instructed me to do.

One other thing that brought me a lot of grief was that my dear friend Fred Lemon's wife had passed away. We attended the funeral of our dear sister, Doris, and little did I know that at this time, when I was having troubles, so was Fred. He felt a cloak of heaviness coming on him; the devil was getting to Fred as well. He was low in his spirit, just like I was.

During December the bitterness had got to the point of no return. The only alternatives were that the devil was going to destroy me or that Jesus was going to sort me out. On Christmas Day I said to Maureen, "I am not going to church this morning." She said, "Ron, it is so important. We must go," but I insisted that, I just wanted to stay at home. This caused a lot of upset in the house. The bitterness was still there; I could not let go of certain things.

On 26th December I became very weak and was getting chest pains. During the following night I became severely ill and was rushed into Basingstoke Hospital in the early hours of the morning on the 28th. I was told afterwards that there had been no hope for me. They had given up straight away; I had suffered another massive heart attack and I wasn't expected to live. Mike Pusey, one of the ministers from my church, had accompanied Maureen to the hospital. When he saw the serious condition I was in he came towards the bed and prayed to the Lord that he would deliver me. He also prayed that the spirit of fear would not come near me and assured me that the whole church would be praying that the Lord would show mercy and raise me up.

Mike left and I was given more morphine, for I was now in terrible pain. I could hear the doctors telling Maureen that this was to be expected because I had suffered so many heart attacks and had coronary heart disease. They told her that I would probably die, and that there was nothing they could do. But Maureen didn't seem to be unduly upset. It wasn't until after the miracle happened that she told me that at that specific time when she and Mike were praying, the Lord had given her a vision of me walking with two people who she assumed were actually angels. I was saying to them, "It only took the Lord two days this time." The miracle and the sorting out in my life was about to begin.

I was lying in the hospital bed, expecting to die. I was quite prepared to die. The pain was now appalling. Although I was given drugs and was on two drips, the pain was getting worse. It was then that the Lord spoke to me in my spirit quite plainly, "It is not me who is doing this to you, it is the devil. You have gone back on our agreement. I called you to do a specific job and you have gone back on that and you have asked me to go out of your life. Now the devil, who has been waiting for his chance, is going to destroy you. I didn't want to allow it, but you have to repent, you have to recommit yourself to what I called you for, before I can help you; otherwise the devil is going to take you."

I remember that for hours I argued with the Lord and said, "Well, you don't understand – all these letters I have been getting, all this back stabbing, all this sneering." Then the Lord rebuked me and said, "Didn't I tell you that you would take up your cross and follow me? What are you expecting? Are you expecting people to stick medals on you? What do you want – to be patted on the back all the time? Do you want to be popular? Don't you like it because you are not popular? Who said you would be popular? Was I popular? The religious people of my day nailed me to a cross. Nobody is going to crucify you!"

The Lord rebuked me in many areas until I felt totally ashamed. I knew I had let the Lord down. After about six hours of arguing and listening to the Lord I repented and prayed to the Lord and said, "Jesus, I am sorry. I know I have let you down. Yes, I tried to be popular. Yes, I did want people to say they loved me and to be patted on the back sometimes, to be encouraged sometimes. But I realise that when one goes out into the front-line to take your message, the devil is going to attack from all areas and you are not going to be popular always, and you are going to get hurt. Who am I to judge other people?"

I realised now that I had been looking at people and not at the sin. The very people that I had started to hate I should in fact have loved. I asked the Lord to forgive me. I just pleaded with Jesus and said, "I am sorry, Lord. I have learned a lesson. I want to take up your cross completely, no matter what the cost, and follow you."

At this time my whole church and many hundreds of people throughout the country were praying for me. After the Lord had finished rebuking me, miraculously the pain instantly stopped. Within two days, just as in the vision that Maureen had received, the crisis was over. The pain had gone, the breathlessness had gone, there was no sign of any damage.

Fred Lemon came to see me. As I have said, I didn't know at the time—he didn't share it with me because, obviously, he was concerned about my illness—but he too was going through a bad time. In a different way from me, but in similar circumstances, the devil was taking him apart. The devil, through the mouths of other people, was telling Fred to pack it in. "You've done enough now," they were saying. "Now Doris has gone, take it easy, call it a day." At the same time that Jesus had delivered me from that heart attack, he was dealing with Fred. He appeared to Fred in his house and spoke to him like a sergeant major, demanding that Fred get up on his feet, for he had work for him to do. Little did Fred and I know, although we had been great friends, that in the near future the Lord was going to bring us together on many occasions and that we would minister together to many people.

The Lord had delivered me. Within two days of the attack I was in the recovery ward and within nine days I was back home again, with no pain. The doctors said I would have to take it easy. They were amazed that I had recovered from this heart attack. This was the sixth heart attack I had had; all the signs were as bad as the worst two and I should have died on this occasion. I have no doubt this was a miracle. I was told that probably I would never be able to do anything in terms of going around ministering, and I would have to take everything completely easy for the next four to six months. But, praise God, the fact is that within six weeks I was back out preaching and I was to see many signs and wonders and an even greater anointing was to come on my ministry.

My first meeting after my illness was at the Ascot Baptist Church on 15th February. The Lord certainly blessed that meeting and the Holy Spirit was very much in evidence. The church was filled to capacity and approximately 100 people responded for various things: healing, salvation, recommitment. This church has grown so much over the past few years due to the faithfulness of their pastor and the willing response of the people.

On 26th February Maureen and Andy Fry, one of the members of our church, accompanied me to Birmingham to a very large Anglican church. This church had received two prophecies a number of years ago that a man from the house church movement would preach from the pulpit and that this would start a movement of the Holy Spirit, not only in their church, but in other churches in the Birmingham area. The church was filled to capacity: approximately 400 people were there, including representatives from about forty churches in and around the Birmingham area.

I was a bit apprehensive about preaching from a pulpit, but the minister didn't want to break from tradition and besides, because of the size of the church, the people at the back would not be able to see me unless I was in the pulpit. I agreed reluctantly, but still felt as if I was in the dock! It raised some laughter when I shared this with the congregation.

I told them a little about myself, and based my message on John chapter 14 verses 12–14. My message focused on the Holy Spirit and on healing and signs and wonders and the need to be free. In our time of worship it amazed us to see how people with ministries of many years' standing received my message. Many people responded to salvation and, to my further amazement, there were 140 in the prayer line for ministry. It took me, together with Andy and Maureen, another hour to minister to them all. We saw people constantly being overcome with the Power of the Holy Spirit; instant healings were taking place; people were being baptised in the Holy Spirit and talking in tongues.

All these things were being witnessed in this church for the first time. During this time of ministry hardly anyone left and because of the signs and wonders they were fervent in their prayer. At the end of the meeting the whole congregation sang "Majesty". Everyone's hands were raised praising God—even those who previously would not or could not. Many were jumping and dancing. Then they stood and applauded Jesus. It is a night that Andy,

Maureen and I not only found hard to believe, but will never forget. Praise Jesus.

Again we see the faithfulness of God. I had a prophecy given to me on leaving hospital. Because I had learned a lesson, not only would I receive healing, but also my ministry would go through a period of change and the Lord would give me a double anointing in my ministry. I know that by God's grace I was lifted up again off that sick bed, yet I had received confirmation from Jesus that the anointing on my ministry would be even greater. I still suffer from angina pains. At times I get angry with the Lord for not healing me completely, but I know that God can use us when we are at our weakest point. I believe the Lord has allowed this thorn in the flesh to keep me under control. I have asked Jesus many, many times to take away the angina because when I get angina pains I get fearful. My only answer is to pray fervently and absorb more and more of the Bible.

I had asked the Lord to remove the pain and everything to do with my coronary heart disease altogether. Then one day he gave me this message from his word: "These troubles and sufferings of ours are after all quite small and won't last very long. Yet this short time of distress will result in God's richest blessing upon us for ever and ever" (2 Cor. 4.17). He also reminded me of 2 Corinthians 12 verses 7–10, where Paul describes how he was afflicted with a persistent ailment which the Lord would not take away, in order to keep Paul from pride and conscious of his weakness and dependence on God. I was given a sickness which has been a thorn in my flesh, a messenger from Satan to hurt and bother me and prick my pride. Like Paul, three different times I have begged God to make me well again. Each time he has said, "No, but I am with you, that is all you need. My power shows up best in weak people." Now I am glad to boast about how weak I am; now I am glad to be a living demonstration of Christ's power. Since I know it is all for Christ's good I am quite happy about the thorn, and about the insults and hardships, persecutions and difficulties, for when I am weak then I am strong. The less I have, the more I depend on him. I praise Jesus for his mercy and for his grace. I have learned a hard lesson.

9. Two Old Lags

It was a dull autumn day late in October 1987 as I motored up towards Norwich. Fred Lemon sat beside me gently singing. On these joint visits Fred prefers me to do the driving because of his age. Since the Lord has graciously provided a car which takes much of the strain out of driving for me, I am happy to serve my old friend in this way.

As the car headed across country, I reflected on God's dealings with me. Like the late autumn trees on the horizon, I had been stripped bare and brought near death three times. But just as surely as the dark hedgerows around me would blossom into life in a few months' time, God had brought me back to life and made me more fruitful than before. "Funny," I mused to myself. "Here we are, two old lags. We've both been in jail; now we're on our way to set the prisoners spiritually free. If you had told me ten years ago that with another ex-convict I would be entertained in the home of a top policeman for the weekend, I wouldn't have been able to cope with it!"

Fred Lemon is an ex-convict whose remarkable conversion story is well known through his books and his many years of ministry throughout the country. He has been one of the main forces in making the churches aware of the plight of prisoners and the work that God has been doing among them. For years a lone voice in the wilderness, Fred is now being joined by an army of converted ex-prisoners like me.

Nurtured in the Methodist Church since his conversion, Fred represents an entirely different tradition from me. However, as we have worked together I have learned to respect the man's integrity and commitment to the Lord. Fred shares his testimony in his own inimitable style. His Cockney sense of humour disarms congregations everywhere and when he prays publicly it is like eavesdropping on a very personal, private conversation. You feel the presence of God. As we have shared together we have learned from each other.

The humility of such a respected older brother in the Lord has refreshed me. It isn't easy for an old soldier like Fred to give place to a younger man, but he has always encouraged and made opportunity for me. At the same time, he has learned from me, just as I have learned from him. God has put us together for a time.

As the car purred on through the cold countryside, I recalled with a smile one of the first times Fred and I had worked together. It was for a "Meet the King" evening at my home church in Aldershot. Mike Pusey, who by then had moved to the King's Church, Newport, came back specially to lead the meeting which he had arranged before leaving for his new charge.

People were rolling in the aisles with laughter at Fred's shrewd wit and the antics which he and I got up to. I don't think Mike knew where to put himself. At one point Fred recounted the story of his baptism. After fifteen years of rebelling against the Lord in this matter, he decided at last to be baptised. This act of obedience blessed Fred so much that when he came up out of the water he cried out "Hallelujah", at which his false teeth shot out. A Christian policeman, Robin Oates, who was at the poolside caught Fred's teeth like an all-England cricketer! In the months to come, I was to become familiar with the phenomenon of

Fred's false teeth. When he gets excited they often shoot out of his mouth. The congregation roared with laughter at Fred's stories and his repartee with me on the platform, but at the end of the meeting at least sixteen people responded for salvation.

The car nosed its way through the traffic and I recalled the 6th July earlier that year, which was a memorable day. Fred and myself were preaching at the tent mission in Crawley Down, which I have already mentioned. My boys had been with us over the weekend and after the Sunday evening meeting I took them back home. Maureen stayed on at Crawley Down because she was due to take a women's meeting on the Monday afternoon.

Before I went, she shared with me that the Lord was telling her to gather some others and begin a nonstop prayer vigil for the rest of that day and through the night. At approximately 3a.m. it was as though the sky around the tent lit up and an angelic being appeared to Maureen and some of the other people present saying, "Go and sleep, the work is done." The power of prayer had opened up Crawley Down to receive the message of Jesus and to expose the evil cults that operated in the area.

Later in the day, Fred Lemon and I returned and in no time were caught up in the enthusiasm and anticipation of the fellowship. Prior to the worship we received a word of knowledge that witches and spiritualists would be at the meeting, so we prayed against this.

I have already described the amazing gathering of people that descended on that little village of Crawley Down. Hundreds of people attended and the sides of the tent were taken down and chairs placed on the outside to accommodate the overflow. In our own way we were witnessing a small revival through prayer.

Near the end of Fred's address I knew he was in

great trouble. He was being attacked physically by the devil. His speech became slurred and muffled and it seemed that the very life was being drained out of him. My spirit told me that Fred was dying.

I glanced to the back of the tent and my attention became fixed on a large woman with very long blonde hair and dark eyes. She was from a spiritualist group and was praying against Fred. At that moment, Fred was about to collapse. I threw a chair under him and asked the brothers to cover him in prayer.

I challenged the woman and told her that if she moved or even attempted to continue her activities God would destroy her. She was frozen to her seat. Another young girl ran out of the tent and Maureen, along with others, challenged her. This girl had been involved with a local satanic circle, but I praise God that Maureen was able to lead her through to Jesus and repentance. Praise God, another of the devil's advocates won for Jesus.

Fred had now recovered completely and the Lord showed us that he had allowed this to happen to prove the truth of what I had been preaching previously. I had spoken of the power of Satan in that area, and in this country as a whole, and how we Christians fail to hit back at him. How little does the average Christian pray to Jesus, let alone pray against the work of the enemy. Yet these Satanists and occultists pray every day in the power of Satan for the breaking up of Christian marriages, for prominent men of God to fall into the hands of sensuous women or for all manner of diseases to fall upon them.

This is exactly what is happening and we Christians are not immune from it unless we put on the full armour of God, take up the battle and fight the evils of this world. By prayer, by faith, by witness, by works, by the total surrender of our lives to the Lord Jesus Christ our Saviour, with the right will and belief we can conquer Satan's kingdom. I know it works—we had seen the start of it in Crawley Down.

In the middle of July, Fred and I went off to the Baptist church at Clare, between Haverhill and Sudbury in Suffolk. The church is led by Dave Whitlock and is beginning to respond to the Holy Spirit. On Saturday evening, Fred and I shared the ministry. We saw 250–300 people in attendance, quite remarkable for a small village. Not only did we see many people blessed and a handful converted, but about twenty young people came forward to be filled with the Holy Spirit and sent out as disciples of Jesus Christ to win folk in and around their area.

On the Sunday morning, we went off to High Point Prison where the two of us spoke to the inmates. As with all the other prisons we have visited, we were amazed at the continuous number of men who are committing their lives to Christ. Our gracious Jesus is putting an army together from the dregs of society. How great and mighty is our God for ministering to these men. We also received tremendous blessing and encouragement for ourselves.

Fred took the morning service at Dave's church and I preached in the evening. I don't think these folk had witnessed anything like it! The people were blessed and set on fire for Jesus. It was an outstanding time, even if Fred did get so carried away on Saturday night that his teeth fell out again!

By now I was turning the car into the outskirts of Norwich where we were to stay at the home of Chief Inspector Barnes of the Norwich police force. I wondered what was in store for us. But there was no need for concern. The Saturday night meeting Fred and I shared was attended by about 450 people. We complemented one another with our presentation of each other's work for the Lord. This resulted in six people being born again and twenty-two coming forward to receive the baptism of the Holy Spirit and to be commissioned to go out and work for the Lord.

On Sunday morning, we were able to go into Norwich Prison. Unfortunately, their most famous prisoner, the jockey Lester Piggott, had already bolted! He had been transferred to High Point Prison which Fred and I had visited a few weeks earlier. Still, if we don't catch up with him I pray that God will. I was sure that many of the men wanted to respond for salvation, even though an altar call was not permitted. I am sure that because seed was faithfully sown, a harvest will be reaped, possibly by the prison chaplain.

Later, in November, I travelled with Fred again as we went north to Forest Road Methodist Church in Mansfield. Our hosts there were Duncan and Judith Shewen. These two precious people, along with their handicapped daughter Heather, became very dear to me as the love of the Lord drew us closer together. I didn't believe that Methodism moved in the things of the Spirit any longer, but how wrong I was. These two are really moving with the Lord, and even have meetings in their home. I knew God had brought me here for a purpose. These people were hungering for the things of the Spirit.

We shared the meeting on the Saturday night to an almost full church, and right away I knew something was going to happen. I knew God was going to do a new thing in this traditional Methodist church because of the obedience of Duncan and Judith and a handful of others. On Sunday morning I preached again on revival and the commitment required to see it take place. On the Sunday night Fred led the meeting and I shared my testimony. The outcome of all this was that we saw people being healed in their seats, others being saved and many, including the minister and his wife and all the leaders of the church, asking for prayer for the spirit of boldness and the baptism in God's Holy Spirit.

We saw a signal outpouring of God's Spirit and a great battle won. Most of the people there said they had never seen anything like it before. People had travelled from Peterborough to hear the good news, because a handful of people were seeking the truth and praying for a release of the Spirit. There was a longing for a breaking of religious traditions, a growing in experience of Jesus and a leading into all truth by the Holy Spirit.

Yes, a Methodist church is going to break the darkness in Mansfield. Not in the power of Methodism, but in the name of Jesus and through the message brought by ex-convicts brought up out of the miry clay. I praise God for Jesus who allowed me to be a fellow labourer with him in the power of his Spirit to be used as a channel to administer his will. Thank God for Jesus who is moving in this and other churches throughout the country.

I received so much love and encouragement over this weekend, and again the Lord showed me, from his word, that he will choose whom he will anoint and use for his glory, whatever the denominational tag. If there are people in a congregation who believe in the full gospel and are hungry for the Spirit and the truth, God is able. He will go forward with the sword of his word in his hand to smash down any obstacle, whether it be denominational barriers or old traditions or stubborn individuals. God shall win and his will shall be done.

As December dawned, I suffered an attack of influenza. Once again I had been overstretching myself. So, almost twelve months after my heart attack, I decided to cancel a projected one week mission in Durham. My body was telling me I needed a rest. I had been looking forward to the time in Durham. However, I felt the Lord telling me not to do it. I have learned over the years never to do things that were not in God's perfect will.

The Lord knew what he was doing, though. Two days later I received a telephone call from Fred Lemon. "Ron," he said, "they've found Charlie."

If you have read Fred's book you will know that Charlie, his brother, went missing twenty years ago after some involvement with the notorious Kray twins in London. Fred had contacted known "hit" men in prison and was told that a contract had been taken out on Charlie's life and that he had been killed.

Fred never completely accepted this information and he, along with others, had continued to pray for Charlie for twenty years. Well, the underground villains may have carried out a killing, but if so they hit the wrong man. Charlie, fearing his life was still in danger, had been lying low and sleeping rough for all this time.

Fred and I went down to Devon where Charlie had ended up in an old people's home. He was very ill and as far as the staff were concerned, there was not much hope for him. But Fred led him back to the Lord and the Lord has his hand on him. Charlie is a little bit deaf and not quite in possession of all his faculties, but he knows the Lord Jesus.

How good the Lord is. He took Fred's Doris home just over a year before. But he then gave Fred back his long lost brother in the closing days of his life so Fred could bring him to the Lord. Fred visits Charlie as often as he can; he is unable to come home since he cannot walk. His legs are very swollen, a consequence of roughing it over the past twenty years. I pray for Charlie, thanking the Lord for his mercy in his life and praising him for listening and answering Fred's prayers.

10. Mountains and Valleys

Ever since I lived in Cardiff for a number of years with my first wife, I have had a love for Wales. In spite of the fact that my experience there was an unhappy one, I always had a conviction that I would go back one day and that the Lord would use me there.

I have consistently found the people of South Wales to be warm and welcoming. There is something, in addition, about the mountains and valleys of Wales that has gripped my heart. Maybe it is because the landscape reflects some of the mountain and valley experiences in my own life. Whatever the reasons, there is a warmth in my heart towards Wales.

I have mentioned my friendship with Dick White-house and his wife, and their local leaders, and how after helping with the mission in Hounslow we were invited to join the fellowship on their holiday later in the summer. The holiday was held at a conference centre called Hebron Hall which is in a small town called Dinas Powis situated between Cardiff and the resort town of Barry. Maureen and the boys came too and we thoroughly enjoyed our time. It wasn't until we got there that I learned that, before being converted into a Christian centre, Hebron Hall had been a remand home for boys. There's a story and a parable in that: God is not only converting convicts, he is converting prisons!

One night, Dick and I went to visit some friends nearby. As usual when you enjoy fellowship, we did not notice the time. When we arrived back at the Hall the doors were shut and it looked as if everybody had gone to bed. We went round the side and found a window on the ground floor which I could open. At which point I got a fit of the giggles. I said to Dick, "I've often tried to break out of the nick, but this is the first time I have broken into one."

It is typical of the Hounslow fellowship that they planned to use the last three nights of the week to conduct a mission in the village. Dick had some Christian friends there who were longing to start a Spirit-filled church. When I learned of their plans I naturally offered to preach. It may have been something of a "busman's holiday", but I am never happier than when preaching the gospel.

David and Josie Neale, who live in Dinas Powis, had booked the Scout Hall for these meetings. When we went to inspect it, we found that there were only sixty chairs in the hall. We challenged them on this. "How many do you expect to get in?" we asked. Because there was a history of spiritual hardness in the village, the faith of the believers there did not extend beyond the sixty seats. Both Dick and I encouraged them to borrow chairs from other churches and eventually we had seating for about 130 people.

At the first meeting there were only about forty-five people present and thirty of those were from our holiday group. Dick led the meeting and announced that God had challenged him from Ezekiel chapter 36 where the Lord said, "Son of Man, prophesy to the mountains of Israel . . . the enemy said of you, 'Aha, the ancient heights have become our possession.'" He said that God had shown him this was true of the mountains of Wales so, then and there, he prophesied to the mountains. The meeting which followed was touched by the Lord and we saw some significant healings. After the meeting a man came up to us and said, "I come from Cwmbran, thirty miles from here.

Did you know that four witches' covens meet on the mountain above our town, though we haven't been able to discover exactly where?"

This brother, named Brian Taylor, edits a Christian free newspaper in the county of Gwent, and was later to become a friend of Dick's. Brian belonged to a fellowship in Cwmbran which was pastored by Bob Yuill, whom I had already met at the High Leigh conference. God was beginning to weave together strands which were destined to affect all of our futures. Bob's church had gone up onto the mountain on New Year's Day to pray against the covens, but they had not been able to locate their meeting place exactly. Brian also said to Dick, "Did you know there is an occult bookshop near to us in Pontypool? The churches there have not been able to do anything about it."

"That is interesting," Dick replied. "That's where I began in the ministry twenty-seven years ago."

The next day Laurence Brown, Amy's father, came up to us and said, "The Lord has shown me that a woman will be in the meeting tonight who will oppose all we stand for, as she is a witch." We had learned to take such statements from Laurence seriously, so we prepared ourselves spiritually.

During the day, Maureen went to speak to a group of women whom she was able to challenge to live for the Lord, and I was interviewed on BBC's local radio station. The interviewer was quite aggressive, and suggested that I was just another American-type money-making evangelist. I told him that if I wanted to be a con man for financial gain I could do it much more successfully out in the world since there were plenty of people willing to spend money on pornographic books and videos. I explained to him that we received no personal benefit from the outreaches in Wales. All the money went on advertising and the hire of the hall.

When I got back to Hebron Hall I received a telephone call from a police officer. He had heard the programme and he told me how impressed he was. He promised that he would be at the meeting on the Friday night with a number of colleagues.

That evening there were about fifty people present and the Lord gave me a powerful message. Then, at the appeal, a woman in the audience started snarling and growling like a wild dog. I have never seen anything like it. Her face contorted and changed shape, hatred burned in her eyes as she leaped towards me. I confronted her in the name of Jesus and she fell to the floor, still spitting and snarling. I wasn't quite sure what to do next. Fortunately, there was a visiting pastor from Bristol present, named Ron McCatty, who had considerable experience in this area. He spoke to the woman quietly but firmly. He addressed not her, but the evil spirit within her and with a calm authority drove it out.

Dick challenged the congregation that there were other people who had been dabbling with the occult who needed to be delivered. Two people came forward. One, a young girl who was supposed to have recently made a commitment to Christ, begged for mercy as we commanded the spirits to leave her. Ron McCatty and I told the demon to stop play-acting and to come out. Whatever it was tried to play on our sympathies, but without success. The girl left, delivered and in full enjoyment of her salvation.

The next morning I was up early and, with Dick and Laurence, headed by car east along the M4 motorway towards Cwmbran. None of us knew the area well. Dick had vague memories of it from twenty-seven years before, but that was all. So we had to rely on the Lord for directions.

We left the motorway and made our way through the edge of Newport towards Cwmbran. "Everything has changed since I lived here," Dick muttered, but he pointed the car in the direction of a sign that said "Henllys". We could see that this was situated on a ridge which must have been the mountain which Brian Taylor had mentioned.

Eventually, we came to a farm entrance, where we asked the farmer if we could get through his farm to the top of the mountain. He explained that there was no access that way, but if we backtracked and took a lane along to the right it would give into a narrower lane leading to a chapel. A little way beyond there we would have to walk.

Following his instructions, we drove up the mountainside until we came to a little Baptist chapel called "Mount Pleasant". In the field behind the chapel we saw a natural stream emerging from the hillside. We climbed over the gate to investigate and saw that there were in fact two streams diverting round a rock and coming together before running into a sheep dip further down the slope. Before us unfolded a view of Cwmbran, Caerleon and Newport with the coastal strip beyond. As we stood there, Laurence began to prophesy. He told Dick and me that God was bringing forth living streams to water the region with his Spirit. We would all be involved in what the Lord was going to do in bringing revival.

By this time I was almost dancing up and down with excitement. Several months before, one of my prayer supporters had shared a vision which she had received from the Lord for me. It was of two streams flowing down a mountainside towards a valley, meeting as they flowed. She also saw a house and she said, "Ron, you are going to live in that valley." I had accepted the vision and spiritualised it in terms of ministry, but now I began to wonder whether it was, indeed, meant to be literal. Here was the very stream that met the description!

As Laurence was speaking, I looked out and it was like seeing a massive desert where suddenly trees and new growth began to sprout. The Lord specifically showed me that Christians from all over Britain would be brought into this area to be part of a new thing that God was going to do. People one would never expect would move location and prominent ministries would be brought into the area.

I did not realise at the time the significance of what God was showing us that day. Since receiving that vision from the Lord, and the prophecy from Laurence, the impossible has happened. Recently, Richard and Margaret Whitehouse with their family have moved into Caerleon, and Laurence and Paula Brown and their children have moved nearby to support them. They have established a ministry team called "Living Streams Ministries" which is reaching out into this and other valleys, nurturing new works.

Around the same time Mike Pusey, my own pastor in Aldershot, moved down to help form the King's Church in Newport. This new church has made its home in a redundant roller disco rink in the centre of town which they have bought and beautifully refurbished. It is capable of seating 900 people and already has a committed nucleus of over 220 people with around 300 in attendance most Sunday evenings. It is becoming a centre of excellence in the new things God is doing and its influence is spreading far wider than its numbers would suggest. Mike Pusey has recently moved on from this ministry and Ray Bevin is now minister at the King's church in Newport.

We proceeded to climb the last section of the lane on foot. This was, humanly speaking, a foolish thing for me to do because of my heart condition, but I felt no undue strain. The lane petered out into a farmyard. We asked permission to go through and, picking up the track on the other side, began to ask directions from the Lord.

We each seemed to be getting specific indications from the Lord which lined up together. We picked up the stream again before it disappeared into the ground and we felt we should follow it to its source. Higher up, the waters emerged from a hole in the ground. We could follow it no further. When it ran out, we could see the peak of the mountain. This was the hardest part of the climb, but I had no angina pains. I seemed to have acquired a superhuman strength. We got to the top of the mountain, but I could detect nothing. I just sat down with Laurence and we started to pray to the Lord. We could see over miles and miles.

Dick proceeded to a cluster of trees just above where we were sitting. He emerged, very excited, saying, "I've found it." We followed him into this clump of woodland and saw a number of stone circles, and it was obvious that this was the site of the coven. We found metal upside-down crosses stuck in the ground which is a Satanist sign. This was obviously the meeting place for a satanic coven. There were enough beer cans and other waste lying around for us to know that it was being regularly used.

We walked around the place praying, and then the Lord said to me, "Just scratch the word 'Jesus' on the ground." And with my bare hands, in the moss and the peat, I scratched the name Jesus. We prayed over it, then left to return down the mountainside. As we were coming down the mountainside I was gripped by a power I had never known. I started to run. My feet didn't seem to touch the ground and I felt as though I was aquaplaning, though I am supposed to have coronary heart trouble. I don't know what speed I was going, but it was as though I literally flew past Laurence and Richard. I got down to the bottom and had to wait quite a while for them to catch me up. I was just full of the joy of the Lord. We were all full of anticipation. We knew we had broken the devil's stronghold in that particular area and we knew the Lord was going to do something spectacular in the meeting that night.

Our final meeting saw the hall packed full. People were sitting on window-sills and standing outside. God's power was flowing over that night. We had delivered the devil a mighty blow and we saw many wonderful things taking place. Many were saved and many were healed. A police sergeant had a deaf ear opened up; people with problems ranging from back disorders, ulcers, blood pressure, asthma and many other ailments were instantly healed. Another man and his wife testified to the wife's healing in her absence on the previous night. We had prayed for her and she was healed at that exact time. She had been in her bed at home with a serious back complaint which she had had for most of her life until the miracle happened. That was also the evening when we prayed for the Browns' daughter, Amy, and for the little boy Gareth.

We left Dinas Powis aware that we had made many new friends and sensing that this was not to be the last time we would visit Wales. In fact, in the months ahead the pace was to quicken so dramatically that Wales has almost become our second home.

Towards the end of April the following year, Dick Whitehouse and I had planned a second outreach with our friends in Dinas Powis. While the meetings were good and we saw fruit, the numbers were not so high as in the previous summer. However, I went with expectancy because on the previous weekend Stephen, my oldest son from my first marriage, had come to visit us for the weekend.

Over the weekend I had shared my faith with him. In the evening we attended the King's Church, where Mike Pusey was preaching. To my joy, Stephen went forward to receive Christ at the appeal, but my joy did not end there. After the service Mike Pusey told me that he had been on a visit to Wales and that while in Newport he had learned news of another son from my first marriage.

On the second night of the outreach at Dinas Powis, I was ministering to some people at the close of the meeting. As I spoke, I was approached by two attractive young women with their children. To my amazement I realised that one was Tina, my daughter from my first marriage whom I had not seen for many years. Her companion turned out to be my daughter-in-law, whom I had never met before. She was the wife of Michael, my youngest son from that first marriage. I had never seen the children until now. This was a very emotional time, as you will imagine. I went back home with Tina and met her husband and was able to share my faith with both of them.

The next day I gained access to Cardiff Prison where I met my son John. I found out that Michael, the son I hadn't seen since he was a baby, was also in prison. They had both been on remand for eight months awaiting trial in connection with robbery and being in possession of a sawn-off shotgun. Because of their records, they expected to receive long terms of imprisonment, but I believe God is intervening in their lives, as he also is in Tina's and Stephen's.

What a legacy of good or evil we leave behind us. Here were my sons following in my criminal footsteps. Because I have turned to the Lord in sincere repentance, and because I am seeking God for them, I believe each of them will also eventually follow in my footsteps, following the Lord. Certainly, they couldn't believe the change that had taken place in me.

A member of Dick's church, moved by this story, began to write to Mike, and he has shown signs of turning to the Lord. At the trial, the boys were sent down for five years, but I know that their faith will be strengthened as well as tested. My prayer is that they will come out on fire for God.

I discovered that I have a total of eleven grandchildren. Jesus has brought me back into contact with my own family whom I had not seen for so many years. I can only believe that it was no accident and that he will work it all out.

In August we returned to Cwmbran to stay with Bob Yuill, who is not only the leader of the Cwmbran New Life Fellowship, but was, at that time, also the Chief Fire Officer for the county of Gwent. We enjoyed lively fellowship with him and his wife Isobel. I had a number of games of bowls with Bob and I must admit that I never so much as won one game. Great things are happening in this area of the country, but I praise God for love, friendship and hospitality which are as much part of Kingdom living as intense and successful meetings. Bob and his wife have become very special friends to me and my family.

In late September 1987 we were back in South Wales yet again. This time there was a team of six of us, including my wife Maureen. Indeed, Maureen was to speak first. On the Saturday afternoon, King's Church, Newport, held a special women's meeting with Maureen as the guest speaker. This turned out to be a blessing, not only to her, but to the many women who responded to her message. In fact, some of their husbands approached Maureen during the weekend to say they didn't know their wives because of the change brought about in them through her ministry.

Once a month, there is an evangelistic rally in Newport, with a guest speaker. These are held in the carpet section of a large furniture warehouse owned by a local Christian businessman. It was here that I was to preach on the Saturday evening.

It was strange to be worshipping amid all the trappings of a furnishing store. Against a back-cloth of rolls of carpet and sales signs hanging from the ceiling, an enthusiastic and lively congregation sang the praises of God. It was easy to preach following the anointed ministry of Charles Graham, a black singer from Tulsa, Oklahoma. Charles is a giant of a man, touched with a gentleness that comes from the Holy Spirit.

As I preached, I felt the power of that same Holy Spirit and I knew before the conclusion of the message that, besides saving people, God was going to confirm his words with miracles. Several people came forward to receive Jesus as Saviour and many were healed.

While I was praying for the sick, a man who was a freelance photographer taking pictures for a local newspaper asked me, "How do I become a Christian?" With great pleasure, I broke off and led him through to the Lord and he received the baptism of the Holy Spirit.

Maureen brought to the front a young woman who had run out of the meeting. She was apparently possessed: her eyes were glaring and she could not say, "Jesus is Lord." She told me, in a voice that was not her own, that voices were constantly telling her to murder her father and mother. The team and I spent some time ministering to her and in the end, praise Jesus, he had the victory. She was set free and committed her life to Jesus.

Barry Stevens, one of the team, followed this woman up. He witnessed a total transformation in her over the next twenty-four hours. Her haggard face was now aglow with the presence of the Lord and she looked years younger. You have to see a miracle like this to believe it. I thank God for the privilege of witnessing him at work and being available as a channel to release his saving, healing and delivering power.

Next morning I preached at Bob Yuill's fellowship. My message was about revival, and there was a remarkable response from the congregation. The evening at King's Church, Newport, completed an action-packed weekend. The Holy Spirit was present in a special way as once more we saw people respond to the invitation to set their lives right with God and to become part of his Kingdom.

During the preaching I forgot my notes and I sensed that there were people present who had been deeply involved in the occult. After I issued a challenge along these lines, four people came forward to denounce Satan. They were each born again and baptised in the Holy Spirit.

Since then, we have visited Wales on a number of occasions. The most recent was for a three-centre outreach in the Rhondda Valley arranged by Dick Whitehouse. We found the pastors helpful and the people welcoming, but we became aware of what tremendous spiritual barriers there are to break through in the valleys of South Wales. Years of exploitation and depression have led to a tight community network. Community relationships have been, socially speaking, the saving grace in the valleys. But, spiritually speaking, they have led to a communal independence, fighting off the rest of the world. The result is a satanic hold which is difficult to break through.

Once again my spirit was stirred within me with a vision for tent crusades throughout these valleys. I believe that God wants me to be involved. The problem is knowing when. I have longed to move to South Wales to live and minister, but each time I ask, God seems to be saying, "Not yet." I know that to make this move would seem like madness. It would necessarily involve foregoing a great deal of the itinerant ministry around the British Isles which brings in most of our financial support. But I have long recognised that God is able to meet every need. I have so often proved the truth that God's will cannot lead us anywhere where God will not provide.

It is my conviction that if and when the move comes, it will involve a change of ministry. Probably it will mean consistently preaching the gospel in a relatively few situations. I believe God is calling me to invest my time not only in preaching, but also in helping others to build the Church.

At the moment, I seem to be in the valley of decision. God's time is not ours, but his timing is always perfect. We are waiting, but whether, as I believe, it is to be Wales, or whether it is to be Timbuktu, God will take us into our next location not just for our benefit, but to fulfil the next stage of the calling for which he has anointed us. He is the leader and we are ready to respond to him.

11. God's Provision

The night was cold and black as we rumbled up the motorway in our battered old Chevette. The headlights stabbed into the night, picking up the reflection of the cat's-eyes ahead of us. I shivered momentarily, for the car heater wasn't as effective as it could have been. Maureen chattered on to me. We were elated after our visit to the Christian Union at the Agricultural College near Cirencester. The meeting had been successful and afterwards we were counselling until very late. Now it was after midnight and we were heading home, making towards Reading along the M4.

Suddenly the car lurched and I heard the familiar slapping of rubber on the road. We had a puncture. Annoyed at the delay, I jerked myself out of the driver's seat to take a look. The offending tyre sat accusingly flat as the wheel settled onto its rim. Wearily, I walked round to the boot to unhook the spare. It too was flat. It must have sprung a slow puncture without me noticing it. I got back into the car, angry with myself for not having checked the spare earlier in the day.

"What do we do now?" I asked Maureen despairingly. We both took a deep breath and thought for a moment. We weren't members of any motoring organisation – we couldn't afford the membership fee. There was no way we could take on the expense of calling out a breakdown vehicle at that time of night either. So we decided to drive gingerly on the flat tyre in the slow lane to the next motorway exit. It would be a distance of some five miles, a risky undertaking, but I couldn't think of anything else to do. "Pray, love," I muttered to Maureen between clenched teeth as I switched on the engine.

Cautiously, I slipped the car into gear and pulled off the hard shoulder. I expected to have difficulty keeping it on track, but the steering didn't seem too bad. Surprised, I picked up speed. I tried the old Chevette at thirty miles an hour. We couldn't hear the slapping of the tyre on the road. I looked at Maureen with raised eyebrows. Carefully, I took the car up to forty and then maintained a steady fifty miles an hour until we reached the exit. I daren't stop to get out and inspect the tyre, but Maureen said, "I do believe the Lord has mended our puncture!"

We kept on going towards the next turn off, pulled down the slip road at the Reading exit and drove the remaining nine miles home without further trouble. The next day the tyre was still intact, but we had definitely sustained a puncture the previous night!

Although we praised the Lord, we realised that we could not expect a miracle every time something went wrong with the car. We had to admit that the old car was coming to the end of its useful life. A puncture could happen with any vehicle, but the Chevette was noisy, bumpy and unreliable. Driving it sapped my nervous energy although it raised my faith levels! However, it was no good turning up to meetings often sweating, dishevelled and late because the car was giving problems.

One Sunday morning at church, I was talking to Ben Benson, a real man of faith in God. "Ron," he said, "you should be praying for a car, a good car, a reliable car. You shouldn't be going round in bangers. That is not honourable to God and he doesn't want you to have it."

I told him, "I am doing okay, Ben. It will be all right."

"No, it is not all right," Ben said firmly. "The reason you haven't got is because you haven't asked. It says in the word if two of us agree on anything in God it will be done. So let's agree you are going to get a new car."

Ben is not a man to take no for an answer, so just to pacify him I agreed. I said, "Fair enough, Ben, we will agree that I will have a car. But I haven't got the faith for a new one. I will agree for a good secondhand car." Ben agreed, but persisted, "We will tell the Lord what make you want."

I didn't know what to say, but Ben isn't easily put off. I remembered that for a very long time, Michael, my son, had been praying to the Lord for a car for me. In fact, he had been praying for a Rover. He had pictures all around his bedroom of a Rover 2600 series 2, which he had been praying that the Lord would provide for me. I certainly didn't have the faith for that, but my son felt that was what I needed, so he was praying for that. So to keep Ben quiet I said, "Okay, Ben, a Rover 2600."

The next thing Ben said was, "What colour?" I began to laugh. He said, "I am serious. What colour?"

I looked round for inspiration. The interior of our church is mostly painted green. It was chosen because, as Phil Greenslade, one of our ministers, is fond of saying, it must be God's favourite colour because he uses so much of it! So to keep Ben happy I said, "All right, Ben, we agree that it is going to be a Rover 2600 Series 2, and it will be green."

He said, "Fine," so we prayed together, but I did it more for Ben's sake than because I believed it. Nevertheless, we said the prayer and I now know that often this is God's way of providing. Sometimes when we haven't got the faith for things, he will use other people with the faith to get things for us that he knows we need.

One day, I had a lot of studying to do, so I decided to take Maureen over to her mum's for company because she knows I like to be quiet and on my own when I am preparing for meetings. I dropped her and the boys off and started for home, but on the way home the car started to overheat and give me trouble again. I pulled into a garage in Hook, a little village just up from where we live, in order to let the engine cool down. I got out and started to walk around, and noticed that on the forecourt there were a number of cars for sale. My eyes just focussed straight in on, you guessed it, a Rover 2600 Series 2 in a metallic green. As I looked at it, I was sure God was saying, "This is your car." I couldn't believe it. It was an immaculate car, only five years old, in perfect condition with only 45,000 miles on the clock. The salesman came over and said, "Are you interested, sir?" I said I was just looking. He went through the usual sales procedure: "Well, just sit in and see how you feel. Would you like a test drive?" He went on with his sales patter and then I said, out of curiosity, "How much would you give me for my old Chevette?" I thought he would refuse to take it, but to my surprise he said he would give me £500 part exchange. I couldn't believe this. That meant I needed another £2,500 if I was to have this car. I told him I would think about it.

I went home and later picked Maureen up from her mother's house. I told them what had happened in the garage and about the car, and we decided to stop on the way home and have another look at it. The boys and Maureen agreed that this was the car God wanted me to have. Maureen said, "You should know by now that what God wants you to have, he will provide the finance for if it is his will."

110

And then the miracles started to happen. It is not my imagination. I never told anyone again that I needed money, but out of the blue a cheque for £1,000, then another for £500 came from the same couple from a church in Winchester that I had visited months before. They wrote saying that God had told them I had need of this money. They didn't know what it was for, but knew I was to have it. So there was the money provided. The other money I needed to make up the balance was also available, but I still had qualms, for I felt that the Rover was a bit showy to drive around in. What would people say? This is how the devil sometimes gets at you. I kept thinking, "What would people say seeing me run around in a car like this? Would they say here was the old Ron again?"

So before I went any further I decided, "Lord, if this is right then I am going to check it out with our finance man at church." I had learned to come under authority now and I knew it was good to check things out. That way you always know if you are in God's perfect will.

I knew Peter Gaut, our finance man, was a genuine person and he would give me a genuine answer. I explained to him the whole story of what had happened. Then I asked, "Do you think this is right? Do you think it is God's will that I should get this car?"

Peter said, "Ron, if it was a brand new car it might look a bit showy, but it is a secondhand one and for that price it is a gift of God. It is worth quite a lot more than that and I believe that if you are going to continue to drive long distances for the Lord, he wants you to have a car that is reliable."

I went back to the garage and gave them my old car and the outstanding money. I shared with the sales representative what had happened and how God had provided for me. He said, "Well, I had better play my part in this," and not only did he have the car totally checked over from top to bottom and give it an overall service, but he also guaranteed it against any mechanical faults whatsoever for a year! Since I have had that car it has given me no trouble at all. I tell people wherever I go, "This is God's car," and explain how the Lord provided it for me.

Although our family had been Christians for a number of years and our love for the Lord was growing day by day, we were experiencing a lot of pressure through continuing to live in the same house where we had known such misery and degradation. Although we knew that everything was clean and new again, just as we were, even as we grew in the love and knowledge of the Lord Jesus and of sins being forgiven, over the years the pressure of living in the house increased and we really had to work hard in our Christian walk with Jesus while in the house. We took our problem to the leaders of the church and Derek Brown himself felt it was right that we should move. We looked around and, try as we may, we just could not find a place anywhere near to the church that seemed to be right. We weren't getting the right feedback, God wasn't speaking to us, and at last I said to Maureen, "I feel God is saying we have got to buy the council house we are in. It is going to be a means of setting us on the first rung of the ladder of having finance." Maureen didn't feel right about this, but I went ahead and got the council to come out and value the house. They valued the house at £39,000 but, because of the fact that we had lived in it for eighteen years, they were prepared to knock £17,000 off which would bring the cost down to £22,000 which we could have on 100 per cent mortgage over twenty-five years. Somehow this felt right to me and I felt we should buy the house on those terms, but Maureen was pretty adamant. She said, "No, I just can't live in this house for another five years, Ron." Regulations at that time stipulated that when you bought a council property you couldn't sell it for five years. So we didn't go ahead with buying the house.

Some months previous to this, Alan Richardson from the King's Centre had moved down to the Dorset area where he was involved with a number of small churches, bringing them together under a new movement called the New Life Fellowship. This was tremendously successful; many people were being drawn to these numerous churches throughout Dorset in Corfe Mullen, Blandford, Poole and other areas. It was during this time that I was invited by Alan to participate in a number of outreaches into the schools and youth clubs and a number of the small churches that were involved in the New Life Fellowships. We saw many tremendous things happening at these meetings.

At one such meeting, a special women's meeting that Alan had organised, Alan and I decided that we would be servants for the day and wait on the women, supplying the refreshments at the tea break. We hid away in the kitchen and in the morning session Maureen was the main speaker. When she started to speak I was totally amazed. I looked at Alan and said, "That is not the woman I married. That is not the meek and mild Maureen I used to know, who was too frightened to talk to even one person. Who is that woman up there speaking like that? She is speaking in some power I have never seen before." It was the power of the Holy Spirit working through Maureen. Alan looked at me and said, "No, that is not your Maureen. That is something special, a special anointing that Jesus has given." And we both knew then that Maureen also was going to have a ministry in many areas.

One of the many opportunities I had to work with Alan was at the Poole Arts Centre. It was the first time I had ever worked in a big theatre. On the very first night I was there, we were in the dressing rooms at the back and I emerged to see a gigantic audience. It was pretty frightening. The seats just disappeared into the darkness from the floodlights and the theatre was packed with people. I remember looking down into the front row at Maureen and she was crying her eyes out. Afterwards, she told me, "I was crying out of pride for you. I was so proud of you, of where you had come from and what the Lord had done in your life. There were hundreds and hundreds of people who had come to listen to you, an ex-convict. I knew what you were, Ron. I married you. Only I know how bad you were, but I was so proud to see how Jesus had changed you and was using you, and people were coming full of expectancy; expecting to see people set free, healed and delivered and to see people give their hearts to the Lord."

On one particular occasion while working with Alan we saw up to forty people make decisions for Jesus, and other miracles happened. Not only Alan and the leadership, but all his fellowship seemed to have a great rapport with me; there was a lot of love there. Because of this love and, as I realise now, the pressure of wanting to move from the house, we came to believe that we had a call to go and work in Poole. We prayed to that end with the members there that God would open up the door for us to move. There was no way that I had finance to buy a house in Poole, so we believed that we should put our names on the national computer for a house exchange. We were hoping that if we were in God's will someone would make a council exchange and it would be a way of moving out. We placed our names on the national computer and it was there for many, many months, but nothing moved, we got no answers at all. We were desperate, for we really believed this call was from God. We were receiving what we believed were prophecies at the time and we were so sure in our minds. It is so easy for us to get into the flesh. You can get a good idea, but it might not be God's idea at all.

I went to meet with Derek and Mike Pusey and told them that I felt we had a call to move to Poole. Derek said that he didn't feel right in his spirit to release me. He didn't think my reasons were right and he felt there was a little bit of hesitation on my part. Today I thank God for men such as him who have the ability to stand up and tell you the truth. It is great to come under their authority, and this is what Jesus said. It is right that we all come under the authority of the leadership of a church, and I thank God for the leaders under whose authority I came. They are full of wisdom and I thank God that I have had the sensitivity to listen to them. After Derek had said that in his opinion it didn't seem right that we should go to Poole, that dashed our dreams of moving to Dorset. And then I did what I should have done before, and that was to pray to the Lord. "Okay, Lord, I believe you don't want me to stay in this house. You know the hurt and the struggle that we go through and that things are not going to be really right for us until you move us or we know we are moving, so let your will be done."

After a while I said to Maureen again, "I do feel that God wants us to buy this house we are living in." I had felt the Lord say, "I am going to give you £17,000," which was the value of the reduction that had been agreed after the council's valuation of the house. And I now believed it was right that we buy the house. In the end we prayed about it and Maureen relented and said, "Okay, go and talk to the council." The next day I went into the council offices to see the Director of Finance and he said that although we had let this lapse for a year and really there should be a revaluation on the house, in fact he would still let it stand at the original price of £39,000 with £22,000 outstanding after the £17,000 was taken off. That in itself was a miracle, for there should have been a revaluation on this property. Then came the shock.

The council official said, "Since your first application over a year ago, Mr Sims, we have looked into your medical records and it would be impossible for us to give you a £22,000 mortgage. The largest mortgage we could give you would be £12,000." They would require a £10,000 deposit and the rest could be spread over fifteen years.

I turned to walk out of the office. My first thought was that there was no way I could raise £10,000. We were just managing on my £76 a week pension and the £42 a week that Maureen earned in her part-time job, plus the little bit extra from family allowance. The two younger boys were still at school and Graham was unemployed at that time. There was no way that I was going to be able to afford this deposit.

As I turned to leave the office I heard the Lord say to me, "This is the house I want you to have, so tell him you will take it." Without really knowing what I was doing I just said to the chap, "Okay, I will take it." He asked, "Have you got the £10,000?" and I said, "Yes," although I hadn't. I wasn't lying: I felt the Lord telling me to say yes. Sometimes we have to make a move in faith if we believe God is saying something. In the world, seeing is believing, but in God's world believing is seeing. I was believing that if this was God talking to me then he would come up with the finance. The next thing the council official asked me was the name of my solicitor. Of course, I didn't have one. Then I remembered the name of a solicitor I had met who had become a good friend. He was a member of the Farnham chapter of the FGBMFI,

Chris Stanbury, and his offices were in Fleet, so I gave the council man his name. He wrote the name down and said, "Very well, if you can see your solicitor and get him to send the necessary papers in and do the necessary search, the house is yours."

So I went along to Chris Stanbury's office, not expecting him to be able to meet with me, but in fact he did and for the first hour Chris and I enjoyed fellowship together, talking about the Lord. Chris is a very elegant and a highly educated man. But he is really down to earth as far as the Lord is concerned. We shared about the great blessings we had received from the Lord and some of the things that had happened in my meetings. And then he asked what I was doing there. And I told him I believed the Lord wanted me to buy my council house. I told him about the £10,000 deposit and that owing to my medical records they wouldn't accept that I believed the Lord was going to keep me alive. So he said, "Have you got the £10,000?" My answer again was, "Yes." So he said, "Fair enough. I will do the necessary search and initial paperwork which should take eight to ten weeks, by which time I will need the £10,000 deposit and then the mortgage arrangements can go through."

I went home and told Maureen what had happened and she said, "If God wants us to have this house then we will see." In the next twelve to fourteen weeks we saw the miracle. We never shared with anybody that we needed finance or that we were going to buy our house. We just left it to the Lord and believed in him, and supernaturally the money started to come in. One fellowship in Wimbledon alone gave me a cheque for £1,000 when I completed a week of outreach meetings there. I queried this. "I think you have made a mistake. There are too many noughts on there," I said. They replied, "No, that is what God told us to give you." Various other monies came in by post from all over the place or were put through our letter box. One night, when I went to read my Bible, I found a pile of ten pound notes inside. To this day I have never found out who put that money in there. I believe it is quite possible the Lord himself could have done that, just as he put the gold coin into the mouth of the fish for Jesus to pay a tax demand. Over the next twelve weeks the full £10,000 exactly came in. I duly went back to Chris Stanbury with the money and the deposit was made and the house was going to be ours. There was no doubt this was God's will and we were on the first rung of the ladder towards buying our house.

Maureen was still a bit concerned about the fact that we had to stay in the house for five years. We knew the value would go up over that time and there would be quite a substantial amount of money allowing us to move. But we continued to pray about this, for it caused us great concern. And again we saw another tremendous miracle. Within the next three months a new law was passed in Parliament decreeing that tenants who had bought their council house could sell the house after three years instead of five. And so it meant that within three years the house would be ours for us to sell and receive the finances that we would need to be able to move, if we were to move, and above all to move to where God wanted us to be. We believed it was God now taking charge. Instead of Ron doing it his way, God was doing it his way.

My ministry was continually growing and I was booked up for months in advance on visits to schools, prisons, churches, celebrations and outreach meetings. With this came the extra volume of postage: letters from people who had made a response at a meeting asking what was their next move, what church they should go to and so on; people asking advice for all sorts of situations they were in, and for members of their family. Also came letters of testimonies of healings and of miracles. I had letters from prisoners that needed to be answered individually.

I had dozens of files and there were papers just about everywhere, stacked up in the corner of our little front room, next to the desk where I used to do all my work. Many times I would spend six or seven hours, right through the early hours of the morning, answering letters, and I knew my filing was not as efficient as it could be. I didn't have any secretarial skills or knowledge of administration as far as office work was concerned, and my correspondence had become hopelessly muddled. Many of the wonderful letters I had from people, testimonies of salvation and healing, have been lost because of the great volume of paperwork. There was just no way that I could keep it or store it all.

On top of this there was the money that all my correspondence was costing me for postage stamps and stationery. The phone bill used to be colossal because of the many phone calls I had to make, answering people who would phone me about problems, and contacting various people. The petrol bill was also mounting from travelling to different parts of the country to attend meetings, to visit or counsel people, to see people in prison. The cost of my ministry was mounting up and I was running into debt. We were selling various things in the home to meet the bills. I was sure this wasn't God's will, but it seemed only a matter of time before my whole ministry collapsed under the weight of the paperwork and the finance problems. There was no way I could go on.

But you see there are some times where we have to learn to make our requests known to the Lord. I find it easier to give than to receive, but I thank God for my dear friend Jim Clark, who is my regional pastor from the church. On one of his usual Thursday visits I was able to explain to him the mess I was in. I said, "Jim, the ministry is just so big now I can't handle the filing, the postage, the letter writing and studying and preparing myself for the meetings as well. It is getting too much. Then there's the cost of the postage and phone calls. And there isn't enough room in my front room to operate from, not to mention the disturbance with all the family activities going on, as you can imagine."

Jim said, as usual, "We will pray about it." We prayed about it and as Jim said, "we made our requests known". After we had prayed, Jim said he would go back to the leaders and talk to them at the next pastoral meeting. Obviously Jesus had it in hand. It is so easy to take our eyes off the Lord, but we need to remember that where God guides he provides. God was guiding me into a bigger ministry and he is not a God of confusion; he was going to make the provision so that ministry could be met. I do thank God for the privilege of being a member of the King's Church, where the leaders are always open and responsive to what the Lord is saying. Jim in due course spoke to the leaders about my problems and they agreed to make two offices available for me: one for myself and one for a secretary. They also provided an electric typewriter, filing cabinets and filing systems. They promised that whatever stationery I needed would be made available, all postage would be paid, and there would be a photocopier for me to use. They also agreed to pay my telephone bill and to provide some financial assistance towards the running and upkeep of my car.

This was an amazing answer to prayer. I could not believe it when I heard what these men of God had done for me. My leaders have been Christians for many, many years and there was I, a relatively young man in the Lord. But they were listening to what the Lord said, and they believed that the Lord was using me and was going to expand my ministry. What a privilege it is to belong to a church like that where the leaders back you not only in prayer, but in finance. The whole church has always backed me, the whole membership have supported me and prayed for me.

Eventually, Rita Horton, a church member whom I have known for some time, agreed to be my secretary. Rita is someone who gives all her time freely to the Lord. Sometimes we have to learn that we have to make a deposit into God's bank before we can make a withdrawal. Rita was giving all her time for nothing, even through the hard times. Now the Lord was seeing that the deposit was made, the withdrawal could come. Many people only look for the withdrawals, but they are not prepared to put in a deposit in times of financial stability. Over the months Rita has been a tremendous encouragement to me.

Because of her, I now have a really efficient filing system: every letter, every testimony that we receive in the office is filed away in its specific file. Every week Rita and I meet to answer all the letters received from new converts, from people in prison, people who write in by the masses from all over the country with various problems. And we have been used by the Lord together to bring comfort and relief and love to many, many people in different parts of the world of all denominations. We have acquired almost 100 intercessory prayer partners and every month we write a prayer letter to all these intercessors, reporting details of the work we have been involved in.

At this time I had a great honour bestowed on me. I was asked by the leadership of the church to become an associated ministry of the King's Centre. Being recognised as an associated ministry of the church would open up more doors for our work. I praise God for these leaders, not only for their belief in God, but their faith in me as a co-worker in the various ministries God has given us. I thank God for Rita, my secretary, without whom this ministry could not function in the professional way it does. But God is a rewarder. He is no man's debtor. Rita's heart's desire was to see her husband Bert become a Christian. Together in the little offices we had prayed and, with the prayers of others, we have seen Bert come home to Jesus. How great is our Lord that he has united this marriage not only in earthly terms, but also in heavenly terms. Rita knows now that she and Bert, just as Maureen and I, can never be parted for an eternity. How great and wonderful is our God and how great and wonderful are his provisions for us.

Besides making provisions for myself and the ministry he has given me, the Lord has also made provisions for, and bestowed tremendous blessings on, the other members of my family. Earlier, I mentioned that my adopted son, Graham, was unemployed. To understand the full story of his life you need to read my first book *Flying Free*, and Maureen's own book *Looking for Love*, where you will hear of his tremendous conversion.

Graham has always been somewhat mentally retarded. He was written off at school; he used to attend a special school and they said he would never achieve anything. But he has great faith in the Lord and over the years after leaving school, although he would only last for a few weeks in a job before being dismissed because he was not up to the work, he would never give up. He always had the belief that the Lord would heal him totally and sort his situation out.

For the last six years, every morning, as soon as he has got up, Graham has read Psalm 91. He literally knows it off by heart and he has claimed the promises of God for healing in his body. And over the years we have seen a tremendous miracle in Graham's life. He has learned to read and write and it is now hard to distinguish him from other people. You can relate to him, you can talk to him on any subject. His greatest hobby is football. He is a great supporter of Aldershot Football Club and goes to their matches regularly. He knows just about everything concerning the history of most football clubs.

The Lord has honoured Graham. Although he tried for years and years to get a stable job without much success, over two years ago he got himself a job with John Adams Caravans as a yard maintenance man. This involves cleaning out the caravans, preparing them for resale, and various other jobs. The management there really loves him and he earns a proper wage. He contributes to his keep and to the household budget, which has been a tremendous help.

Our middle son, Michael, left school and went straight into an engineering job. He didn't get on too well there, so then he went into catering, working at a local hotel. The only problem was that this involved split shifts. That meant he worked four hours in the morning, then he would come home for a few hours and go back at 6p.m. to work until 11p.m. and sometimes midnight. He would be rostered for a couple of days off here and there, but usually he would have to work every Sunday morning and sometimes Sunday evenings which meant he would have to miss the service at church. He didn't like this because Michael loves the Lord and attendance at the church on Sunday mornings is an important part of his life, as it is with all the family.

This was hurting Michael. One day he came home at dinner time and said, "Dad, I don't want to be out of work because I want to be able to pay my way. I don't know what I can do." I said, "Son, there is only one thing to do. We have got to pray about it. We must make our requests known to Jesus." I always encourage my family to make their requests known to the Lord, no matter what the situation or problem is, because God has the answer to all our problems. So we sat down together and I said, "Son, let's tell the Lord what you want." I got a piece of paper and a pencil and said, "Right, what kind of job do you want?" Michael said, "Dad, I would like a nine to five job, five days a week because I would like Saturdays off so I can go to football with Graham, and Sundays so I can go to church." So I wrote that down. Then I asked, "What kind of money are you looking for?" He said, "I would like to clear about £70 a week. I think that is pretty fair. I don't think that is asking too much because I would work hard for it." Our next move was to go into the Job Centre. We looked around and there on the board was a job advertised for a stores assistant in Gateways supermarket, directly opposite the Job Centre. We went to the manager in the Job Centre and he filled out an interview form.

Michael went over to Gateways and had an interview. He took along two references, one from our local policeman and one from Jim Clark at the King's Church, and he was given the job. It involved work from 9a.m. to 5.30p.m. and he cleared £70 per week. What we asked the Lord for, Michael received. Today, Michael is working in catering again, but his present job does not involve weekend work, and he is happy in it.

So, God has provided not only for me and for the ministry, but also for my family individually. With the lads now at work bringing in income besides the pension I still get, the financial situation over the years has gradually got increasingly better. This has meant that Maureen has been able to give up her part-time job. In fact, she needed to give it up because so many doors were opening up for her too in her own ministry. She regularly comes with me on most of my prison and other visits, but she also takes many church meetings of her own. Indeed, she is one of the very few women who have been used as a speaker for the FGBMFI.

In her meetings, and through the ministry that God has given her elsewhere, Maureen also has seen great fruit for the Lord as far as seeing souls saved and bodies being healed. Her autobiography, *Looking for Love*, has recently been published and I know that it will prove a tremendous blessing and encouragement to many. God has given Maureen an individual ministry as well as being part of a joint ministry with me. I just long for the day when the family are grown up enough, and the time is already in sight, when we can travel the length and breadth of this country, maybe to various parts of the world together, as a joint ministry spreading the good news of Jesus Christ to all those lost souls. I know and will always know above all, that wherever God guides he provides. And my God will supply all my needs according to his riches in glory.

12. Home Base

The car swung smoothly through the village. I turned off the main road and rounded the bend into Mitchell Avenue. There were some good meetings behind me. I was tired but happy, enjoying a sense of fulfilment. Still, it was always a good thing to come back home. Home is a haven of peace and acceptance in a turbulent sea of activity, and I always look forward to being with Maureen and the boys again. Though now I reflected that things had been a bit tense at home recently. Maybe it was time to ease up on preaching commitments for a while. Nevertheless, it was good to be back.

As soon as I entered the house, I sensed that something was wrong. As I moved towards Maureen to kiss her, I could see from her face that everything was not as it should be. "What is the matter, love?" I asked. She turned, picked up a letter and said, "I think you had better read this."

The letter was on official headed notepaper from David's school. David, our youngest, has always been too much like I was at his age for comfort. For this reason I tended to be harder on him than the other two. Now, as I looked at the letter, I could see that my fears had been justified. David was suspended for getting into a fight, breaking another boy's nose. Even worse was the implication in the headmaster's words that I didn't care. David was not to be allowed near the school again until I consented to see the head. I gritted my teeth. "What does this mean?" I shouted angrily. "Where is he? Let me get at him."

Slowly, the story came out. For several weeks David had been getting into trouble at school. Maureen had covered up for him, hiding the notes or answering them herself. She was afraid of what my reaction would be and concerned that it might take my mind off the work to which God had called us.

My explosion of anger confirmed her fears. She attempted to calm me down, but I was too angry to think clearly. I saw David following the same path that I had and I desperately wanted to prevent it, yet here I was bursting to behave towards him exactly as my mother used to behave towards me! The veneer of sanctification had worn thin.

"What must the school think?" I fumed. "They know my story. I've been there to speak to assemblies and to the Christian Union. How can I lift my head up in front of the headmaster and staff again?"

If only I had known. This was part of the problem. David had taken a lot of stick because of me, taunts because of what his dad had become, sniggers of "holy Joe" aimed at him. There had been times in the early days when he had stood up for the truth. Faced with a religious education teacher who told the class to write alternative explanations for the miracles of Jesus, he bravely stood up in class and said, "There are no alternatives. What Jesus did was real." He bore the brunt of a lot of sarcasm for that.

The trouble was that I hadn't been around to hear what he was going through. And, if I had, my attitude would have made it difficult for him to share it with me. My standards were high because I didn't want him to slip. Consequently, he was afraid to show his dad any signs of weakness or failure. As a Christian father I was failing simply because of my anxiety to succeed in this area. Satan is so subtle. He knows how to destroy family unity.

After our much publicised conversions and my entry into the ministry, both David and Michael, who is eighteen months his senior, were put under a lot of pressure, socially and at home. At school they were expected to behave well just because of what their father was. I added to this pressure by instilling into them that the way they behave reflected on what I was and what the Lord had called me to do. All the time they were constantly aware that they had to act in certain ways or they would be an embarrassment to me.

I was guilty of trying to force God onto them, forgetting that God has given us all a choice and that we individually have to find our own way with Christ. As a Christian father I have since learned that we can show our children Jesus and set them an example, but we should never attempt to become God to them.

I began to realise these things after I had finally calmed down, got David on his own and allowed him to speak. I could hardly believe what I was hearing.

"Dad, I do believe in God and in Jesus and I do pray, but don't you see? I have no life of my own. Right from six years back you expected me to do this or not to do that or not to say the other because you are a famous person. I had to live life up to your and other people's expectations. I'm David, an individual, not you. I can't be like you and God doesn't want me to be like you. It's hard for any young person in the world today, but it's even harder for people like me whose dad is a well-known evangelist travelling the country.

"It is like being a prisoner, being told what to do and what to say, who I can have as mates, how I can't go here or there and so on. Dad, I feel like a prisoner and you preach that Christ came to set the prisoners free. Dad, I love you. I'm not irresponsible. I know right from wrong. I don't usually get into trouble, but please let me be me. I could kid you on to please you, but that wouldn't be right. Please let me be honest, let me have space. If God wants me to serve him, he will sort me out in his way and his time."

It was an eloquent outburst from a young man who usually bottled things up, and it shook me. Had I really been so blind and insensitive? I thought back to my own childhood and how I had been pressured in very different ways. What David was experiencing was more subtle, but no less real. I didn't want to lose him or to see him go Satan's way, so I gave the problem over to the Lord. I was concerned about Michael too. He is quieter and less explosive than David and less likely to react in the way David had, but I began to realise that he too was feeling the pressure.

Although I had given the matter over to the Lord, my immediate reaction was to feel a failure. I was even tempted to blame God! After all, I was giving my time over to him. Couldn't I expect him to look after my family? How often I have heard thoughtless Christian workers say, "If I spend my time caring for God's children, I can leave him to take care of mine."

Deep down I knew that reasoning was wrong. God does care for our families, but he expects us to pay attention to our responsibilities too, and as a father I knew I was meant to be a channel of God's grace to my boys. Grace doesn't mean rules and restrictions; it means a Christ-like model based on unconditional love. Clearly, I had failed.

Miserable with myself I drifted into the church office and talked to Derek Brown, our senior pastor since Mike Pusey left. He was very understanding and sensitive and gave me helpful advice.

"Ron, you need to spend quality time with your boys, even if it means cutting down on the number of preaching engagements you take. You must learn to do what I do. Keep the boys in mind when you are fixing your diary and make sure you spend one or two days every week in their company. Find out what their interests are and show you are interested. Go and watch football with them, or whatever, but invest time in them. They won't be around for ever. Your first mission field and your first responsibility is your family. If you fail with them, your whole ministry could be discredited."

Instinctively, I knew he was right. I haven't always succeeded, but ever since then I have tried to make more space in my schedule for the family. I realised I hadn't been fair to Maureen either. I had expected her to be both mother and father while I was away, without giving her the backing she needed when I returned. Too often I had returned home exhausted, but full of what had happened to me on the trip and how the Lord had blessed my work. Then, turning to the inevitable pile of accumulated mail, I would forget to ask about family matters. I would forget the responsibility Maureen bore, without the exciting reward of the immediate results I was being privileged to see.

It sometimes takes a crisis before we can hear God clearly about the more obvious matters. During that week I learned some lessons and I learned to listen to God more clearly.

The pressures continued at school, and Michael was feeling it too, with the other youngsters teasing and provoking them, goading them about their father going soft, or that he was a Jesus freak or a "poof". Michael became increasingly nervous and withdrawn, but we were determined to love him through it. We couldn't take the pressures for him, but we could try to understand.

Since Michael left school and settled into work he has been very happy. He is a great son and I am proud of him, as I am of David. He knows the Lord and, although he isn't following him now as closely as he used to, I know God has his hand on him and has a work for him to do. He has a loving and caring nature and once it was prophesied that he will become a pastor. I can believe that, but whatever Michael or David become, I claim for them the promise of Philippians chapter 1 verse 6 that God will complete the work he has begun in them.

David too has now left school. Currently, he is working as a carpet fitter, but I do not believe he has yet found what he ultimately wants to do. Since they left school I have not forced the boys to read the Bible, to pray or attend church. What they do, they have to do because they want to now that they are at an age of accountability.

So many Christian families have split apart because the parents have forced Christianity onto their teen-age children. I have been in Christian homes with problem teenagers where the parents have said, "Either they conform or they leave home and find somewhere else to live." I believe that all the time our children stay with us, no matter what age, we should set standards that they must abide by, but we cannot force our Christianity down their throats.

If they don't want what we represent and we end up losing them, so will God. You can love and pray your problem teenager into the Kingdom. So often we worry about what others may think. It is more important to be concerned about what God thinks and is saying. He is not into seeing families break up, but Satan is. I have learned all of this and I have learned it the hard way.

I sat a few rows back in the church hall in Mansfield. Tears filled my eyes as the shy young man in front of us shared simply but from the heart what Jesus meant to him. "This is a miracle," I muttered to myself as I brushed a tear away. "I would never have thought our son could do this."

The young man was Graham, Maureen's son from her first marriage. To hear him speak so definitely about his faith in front of a crowd of young people filled me with wonder and pride.

I have been Graham's dad since he was a year old. From his earliest years he was backward, and all of his school life was spent in special schools. Before my conversion, I made his hard life even harder for him. I used to tell him he was useless and sick. I am ashamed of the evil and negative things I said to him.

When he left school Graham couldn't read or write. At the age of sixteen he had the mental ability of an eight-year-old, and was unemployable. He then started having epileptic fits. Life wasn't pleasant for him, and at times he reached a point where he didn't care if he lived or died.

Then came the dramatic change. Shortly after my and Maureen's conversion he too became a totally committed Christian. Since then he has grown and grown in the Lord. It was a slow process but, as his love and faith in the Lord grew, so it released boldness, healing and deliverance. He now has a faith which, at times, puts mine to shame.

In the early days, Graham found it hard to mix with people or to get involved with the times of praise and worship when the church met. But God has honoured him and his simple trust that anything he asks in his name, Jesus will do for him.

Over the years his boldness has grown amazingly. A real release for him came at one of our Sunday evening worship sessions at Aldershot. Fred Lemon had joined the family and as we worshipped at the King's Centre the Lord touched Graham. Without any warning, as we were in praise, his arms went up above his head and shy Graham was out in the aisles dancing. There were tears of joy in brother Fred's eyes, along with Maureen's and mine.

As I have already mentioned, Graham had a bad time for years over getting work. He would either be sacked for incompetence or the other men would make his life unbearable, mocking him, especially if he shared about his faith in the Lord.

Graham never became bitter. His answer was always the same: "I can see the Lord didn't want me to have that job – he has got one lined up for me somewhere." He never once doubted God or that he was in control. He also believed steadfastly for the healing of his epilepsy and that the Lord would teach him to read and write. In the past few years all of this has come about. The epilepsy is under control, without medication. He has only had two seizures in the past three years. He is able to read and write. He is now happy in his work at John Adams Caravans, and as far as the management is concerned he has a job for life.

Graham has now stood before a church congregation a number of times to share his testimony to the glory of God. This time at Mansfield was the first time I had been able to be present on such an occasion. No wonder my eyes kept filling up. I was watching someone the world had written off, completely restored by the Lord. Graham is a new creation physically, mentally and spiritually. Every night when he gets home from work he plays a praise and worship tape while he washes and changes. After dinner he is into the word of God. He really does love the Lord in the simplest way, with a child-like faith.

On one occasion he said to Maureen, "Mum, I know Jesus will keep Dad alive and that he won't die of any more heart attacks, but if somehow Satan manages to get in and Dad does have a heart attack and dies, no one is going to take him out of this house. I will lock

134

myself in the room with him and pray and pray until we both walk out together." That isn't bravado. It is a genuine expression of the strength of Graham's faith.

How important the home base is. I nearly allowed Satan to break mine up, caught up as I was in a hectic ministry schedule. Once you get into front-line ministry—"plundering hell to populate heaven" to borrow Reinhard Bonnke's memorable phrase—you become public enemy number one as far as Satan is concerned. His prime target is your family. He will try every conceivable angle, every crack or chink there might be in your armour of faith, in order to get into your family. He will fire darts of deception, disagreement and doubt to bring about arguments and distrust.

We have gone through many traumatic times, but I praise God that he is always faithful, even if at times we are not. When I feel I have let the Lord down in the family area of my life, I am continually encouraged by the promise: "He that has begun a good work in you will perform it until the day of Jesus Christ" (Phil. 1.6).

I'm also a believer that the man and wife who read the word of God together and pray together will be stable. The Catholics had it right when they coined the slogan, "The family that prays together stays together." I have not always lived up to this, and not only because of the times when I am away from home. Whenever we have failed in this area, the enemy has begun to disrupt family life for us. I know this is an area in which many Christian families fall down, but I believe it is God's will that we should come before him as family units, making all our requests known.

I never cease to be amazed by the number of Christian families I meet where there is total disagreement. This extends right down to cases where husband and wife go to different churches with different beliefs and doctrines. No wonder their children are split down the middle in total confusion. God is not a God of confusion, the Holy Spirit is a Spirit of order. Where Jesus truly reigns, there will be a Kingdom order, but Satan is able to work havoc in the disordered family.

13. Behind Every Good Man

They say that behind every successful man there is a good woman. That is certainly true in our case. Without Maureen's backing I do not know how I could have sustained these years of ministry.

For a long time hers was the less exciting, more humdrum task of keeping the home together and looking after me when I have frequently come home exhausted and, occasionally, discouraged. Never once did she complain or cease to believe that God has called us together into a ministry.

I am convinced that this is what sustains her. Not the determination to slog and battle to keep things going so that I can go out and have a good time serving the Lord in more exciting ways. Rather, it is the belief that together we are engaged in two sides of one ministry.

I have always loved taking Maureen out with me when I preach. I never feel more secure in the Lord and in my ministry than when Maureen accompanies me. It is as though our ministry team is more complete.

This is not always easy for Maureen, especially when the demands of evangelistic proclamation cause me to focus on our testimony. She does not savour reliving the past, particularly as much of it was painful for her and in these meetings it is made so public. She finds this embarrassing. I don't relish it either. My main concern is to move the attention from Ron Sims and what he was, onto what Jesus has done. Unfortunately, the one is necessary to achieve the other. Occasionally, Maureen would be asked at this type of meeting to share her side of the story. Although she found this difficult because of the emotions it aroused in her, she always spoke powerfully and effectively.

Unfortunately, as the lads were still at school in the early days, Maureen could only come with me to local venues or on the occasional weekend when there was accommodation for the boys too. Gradually, she has been able to travel with me more often as the boys have become more independent. Even so, they still need our presence and encouragement, so it isn't always wise for both of us to travel. Over the years, there were clear pointers to the future when Maureen would be with me regularly. I also knew there would be times when she would minister on her own account and the boot would be on the other foot. I would be accompanying her or even staying at home to hold the fort.

All through my Christian life and walk with Jesus, Maureen has been a constant source of encouragement, backing and a constant companion. For many years she worked in a part-time job at an antique shop in the village, bringing in the finance to balance the books and to support the ministry God has given me. This, besides running a home and caring for the family.

Over the years as Christians, our love for one another has grown, but it hasn't always been easy. We have had to work at it. I am far from being the easiest person to live with and the pressures of the ministry, and the hurts one often endures, spill over onto the family. Maureen has often acted as the backstop, preventing other people from catching what I am going through.

The evil temper I had before Jesus intervened in my life has gone, but I am still a fiery person. Sometimes, sparks of the old nastiness break out and it is usually Maureen who bears the brunt of it. She seems to be the one earthly person on whom I unload all my hurts, frustrations and anger. I always take my problems to my heavenly Father, but I admit that sometimes it takes a prompting from Maureen first.

I guess I am the same as many men in the ministry. The public see us on the platform with smiling faces, the anointed men of God. But it is our wives who see us come home exhausted, washed out physically and mentally – and sometimes spiritually. They are also the ones who cry with us over some of the nasty comments, poisonous phone calls or letters from religious cranks. I thank God these are now few and far between for me, but Satan will never give up in his determination to destroy the evangelist's ministry. When he gives up one line of attack it is usually only because he is preparing another.

Maureen is an excellent mother. If the upbringing of the family had been left to my blundering efforts alone, we wouldn't have come this far! The family needs a strong lead from a father. The spiritual order is distorted where men are reduced to nonentities completely dominated by their wives. I knew enough of this in my own early childhood. My mother totally dominated my father, even physically abusing him as well as us children, and it was that background that drove me to a life of violence and crime.

The strong husband isn't domineering either. Meekness is the quality which he most needs. I have heard meekness defined as "controlled strength". I haven't always succeeded in this, but insofar as I have, it has been because of Maureen's gentleness and sweetness.

I believe there are too many mothers who are neglecting their children because of the demands of their work. Consequently, on my visits to schools I see thousands of "latch key kids", who have nobody in the house to look after them when they get home. Some of them are as young as seven years old. Their mothers are out at work until six, seven or even eight in the evening. Starved of a mum's affection, left with a snack meal, their whole life centres round a box in the corner of the room with a video machine under it. Small wonder that while mum and dad are out many kids go down to the video shop and hire horror or porno films, or take a few pills. Many children are suffering from affluent neglect. Their future emotional well-being is being sacrificed on the altar of affluence.

The love and care of a mother, backed up by a sensitive and responsible father, is the most potent weapon for lowering the crime rate in this country. You may ask where I get my information from. The answer is, straight from the horse's mouth! As I speak to thousands of young people in remand centres and prisons throughout the country, as well as in schools, I hear hairraising stories of parental neglect.

Satan is breaking down the structure of families and as a result the children of the nation are being destroyed morally, mentally and physically. I pray that men in this country will wake up to their responsibilities in the home. I pray for homes where discipline is not a dirty word, where children are brought up in love and respect for their elders, and women are able to fulfil their role as mothers. This does not mean women should not work outside of the home, but that the family should come first.

In this matter we have taken our own advice. We have been glad of the financial input from Maureen's job, but she arranged to work between 9.30 a.m. and 12.30 p.m. each day so that she could see the boys off to school and be there to greet them when they came back. Even so, we still had problems. Many of these came from the attitudes of families around us which washed off onto our own boys. We only survived out of our determination to work the problems through lovingly.

Graham is now praying for what he considers to be the greatest and most important blessing in his life: a Christian girlfriend and eventually a Christian wife. He is not only praying, but he is saving up to make provisions for her, bless him. I know the model he holds up for this future partner is his mother. I thank God for this because his earliest example from us as parents wasn't so wholesome.

One of the hardest lessons I had to learn on becoming a Christian was how to love my wife. I had to learn to love Maureen physically, as well as emotionally and spiritually.

This was a legacy from the past. Our involvement in the pornography racket meant that I had witnessed the most debauched and debased forms of sexual activity. Illicit sex is like a drug: it dulls sensitivity and it requires increasingly frequent involvement and more extreme forms to achieve the same effect. Because it is indulged in purely for self-gratification it deteriorates into mere physical aggression, and there is no place for tenderness.

Before my conversion, I had become unresponsive to normal sexual stimuli. The naked female form no longer aroused any interest in me. Consequently, when I became a Christian I had lost the ability to appreciate my wife. Displays of affection or tenderness did not come naturally to me. Maureen herself had became a wreck because of the way I had treated her.

This sounds like a recipe for marital disaster and, indeed it was, but when the Lord renewed us, he put into us a new capacity to love. It had to be worked at, but we became like a courting couple all over again. I have surprised myself by the tenderness which God has put into my heart. Right from the beginning, even before the involvement with pornography, my love for Maureen was flawed. As a result of my mother's brutality and my first wife's infidelity, I was unable wholly to love or trust any woman, and I exploited Maureen in many ways. I have had to learn to please her and to take thought for her before myself. In so doing, the Lord has blessed us and caused our love to grow.

I leaned back on the park bench in the spring sunshine, my arm round Maureen's shoulder. We were soaking up the goodness of God's creation around us, content in each other's company. "This is better than our courting days," I thought to myself. "After all we have been through, we don't have to prove anything to each other any more." Feelings of tenderness welled up within me. "It's so good to feel secure with a woman I can trust and who loves me so much," I reflected. "I wish she could be with me more often in the ministry."

Those thoughts and wishes were soon to come to fruition. It had begun with a more public recognition of Maureen's ministry. Before Mike Pusey left Aldershot for Newport, he invited Maureen to give her testimony at the King's Centre there. It was a great evening. Mike finished off the meeting with an altar call and many came forward to commit their lives to Jesus. Since then, and as the boys have got older, her activities have increased. Not only has she joined me on tent missions and in other ministry, she has been used in her own right taking many women's meetings all over England and South Wales.

In January 1988, the Lord told me that Maureen was to give up her job and prepare herself for full-time ministry alongside me as a joint venture. He also showed me that he was going to use her in her own right to reach many young women for Christ. He said that we were to look to him for all our financial needs. As far as the ministry was concerned, it would mean an immediate drop in income of approximately £2,300 a year, so it would be a step of faith, for us.

Although Maureen's greatest wish was to travel with me and to work full-time in the ministry, she was hesitant. She is never willing to act until she has heard from the Lord and I knew I must wait until she heard from him for herself. After all, it is in the mouths of two or three witnesses that the testimony is established.

By now I had a small ministry team of men who often travel with me. When I am at home they meet with me once a week to pray and seek the Lord. On one of these occasions God spoke clearly to all of us that Maureen was to pack up her job and make herself available to the Lord. Not until she made this move in faith would God honour her in the future as far as ministry was concerned. Maureen received this as from the Lord, so in June 1988 she resigned from her job and made herself totally available to the Lord.

We trusted the Lord to make good the loss in finance. The Lord in his word says, "Prove me, now." We did this and he has honoured his word. Since she gave up her job, invitations for Maureen to speak at church gatherings and women's meetings have flowed in. My own publishers brought out her biography recently. God is beginning to open up the doors of heaven as he promised.

God is blessing Maureen for her faithfulness. We are growing daily in our love for each other and in our love for the Lord. Of course, we still have our problems and occasional disagreements, but a quick telephone call to one of the couples in ministry with us, a time of prayer seeking the Lord, and our problems are soon solved. That is the way it should be; when the attacks of the enemy come we need brothers and sisters who can get alongside us. There is a strength in standing together with those who love and understand us and who are committed to us.

It is all a question of covenant commitment. Maureen stands behind me as a support, but also increasingly alongside me as a partner in "up-front" ministry because we are committed to one another in the marriage covenant. This has come to mean more to us as we have matured in Christ. When we first married it was more a question of mutual attraction, personal needs after the failure of our first marriages, and convenience. Although we were married in a registry office, I believed even then that marriage vows were made before God. That did not mean much to us at the time, but since then our vows have become forged in God. You see, there aren't just two of us involved in the partnership now. God has first committed himself to us in the person of the Lord Jesus Christ who gave his life blood for us. Jesus in turn has sent his Holy Spirit into our hearts as a deposit of eternity. Not only is he the Spirit of holiness, he is consequently the Spirit of Christ who dwells in us. Thus we "submit to one another out of reverence for Christ" (Eph. 5. 21). We do it out of reverence for Christ because each of us recognises his presence, by the Spirit, in the other.

Just as the Trinity is a covenanted company of three, so we are covenanted together with the Lord. The Old Testament rightly observes that "A threefold cord is not easily broken" (Eccles. 4.12). With Christ in the partnership, our covenant commitment is able to bear the weight of the stresses which often overtake us.

I am glad that our covenant together is working more and more in terms of a joint enterprise for the Lord. We feel there is strength and a future in this. Neither of us feels unduly concerned about my

144

physical condition, although I am glad that Maureen, as part of her ministry, keeps an eye on my diet, reminds me when I am overdoing it and takes care that I live at a sensible pace. I know that I sometimes make it hard work for her because I am anxious to achieve as much as possible in the time the Lord has allotted me. Having Maureen in harness with me relieves me of some of the load. Maureen and I are both confident that, provided we keep within the guidelines, nothing is going to happen to prevent our ministry fulfulling its course. It will not come to an end before God's time.

14. Where the Buck Stops

As I have been preparing this book for publication, many of us in full-time evangelism have felt the backlash of events in America. I am referring, in particular, to the startling and scandalous revelations about the sex lives of a couple of television evangelists. Both cases were so shocking as to scandalise worldly people, let alone the Church.

I do not condemn these men; far be it from me to throw the first stone. God knows the pressures and temptations when one is constantly travelling, far from home and spending time away from the family.

Chuck Swindoll records in one of his books just one such temptation he experienced in a hotel. Hundreds of miles from home, feeling tired and with his defences low, he was propositioned by an attractive young woman. He records that it took a mental picture of his wife and family, cool determination and earnest prayer to resist the momentary temptation. If such a godly man could be tempted, even for a moment, the rest of us had better watch out.

Up to now this hasn't been my problem, but I have had to face other temptations and difficulties. At the time of the revelations concerning one of the tele-evangelists in America, a colleague rang up and said, "The thing that bugs me is that I have to ask, 'Didn't the man have any close friends to whom he was accountable?'" For me that question has significance for any serious Christian, especially for those of us in full-time ministry with specific responsibilities.

Throughout my story I have acknowledged the fundamental role of the church in Aldershot to which I belong. The church is committed to supporting my ministry and I make commitments to the church. The royalties from my first book are given to it, for instance.

In return, the church gives me office space, secretarial help, a car allowance and, what is more important, recognition. The senior pastor, Derek Brown, now has responsibility for overseeing my ministry. Periodically, I report back and give an account of what I have been doing. The church prays for me and a committed group within the fellowship is given to intercession for our ministry.

It is all a question of accountability. When you are frequently in the spotlight where God is honouring your ministry and is using your gifts, it is easy to act as though you are above the law. Indeed, when lots of people who don't see you very often look up to you because of the effects of your ministry, it could be easy to begin to believe in your own infallibility.

That is where friends come in and accountability begins. Those who are close to me and have invested time and care in my life have a right to call me to account as to what I do with their trust. Primarily, my accountability is to God, but it is easy to become proud and spiritually insensitive, even in the midst of service to the Lord. Or, indeed, especially in the midst of service to God. It is so easy to allow the aura of sanctity around our ministry to extend to everything we do. Of course, everything we do should be equally sanctified, but the reality is that an artificial sanctity can sometimes be attached to ministry. If we are taken in by it, we may come to believe we are never wrong. A wife and good Christian friends are the best corrective to falling into this trap.

When things were going wrong with David and Michael at home I felt like giving up the ministry, but, as I have said, Derek Brown gave me the help and advice I needed. It was also about this time that I met up with four spiritual men who have since been a great source of support to me and to the family: Otto Bellinger, who attends Millmead Baptist Church; Barry Stevens, who is now at Bagshot Evangelical Church; John Sheppard, who attends an Anglican Church in Aldershot; and finally Ian Watson from the Basingstoke Community Church. They are all Spirit-filled Christians who back me in the ministry. They travel with me when they can and if I am away without them, they or their wives keep in touch with Maureen. The fact that they all come from different church backgrounds has proved to be a strength to us. It has never been a cause of difficulty or dissent. In fact, the differences of perspective are a positive help in many of the situations which confront us.

Besides a supportive church, the commodity which people in ministry need most is real friends. Whether they are from the same congregation or not does not matter, as long as they do not override the spiritual authority of one's own leaders. For people whose ministry is in the leadership of a specific congregation, it is even more imperative to have friends to whom they are accountable, preferably outside of their own area of responsibility.

There have been many occasions when we five men have got together, sometimes with our wives too, and the Lord has spoken clearly to us. Times of prayer and seeking God together have been precious to us. It is in an atmosphere of trust like this that I am able to share my weaknesses and uncertainties, knowing that because they are real friends these men will accept me

as I am. At the same time they are concerned to see me
develop and to move forward into greater spiritual
growth.

Real friends are not those who identify with your
success but walk away from your failure. True friends,
like these men, accept and affirm. Because of their love
and commitment it is possible to turn weakness and
failure into success.

The Bible tells us that Christians should submit to
one another. Submission is a Christian discipline
out of which comes great strength and maturity.
Nevertheless, the biblical practice of submission is
not based on a military model. It comes out of trusting
relationships.

When the centurion came to Jesus wanting his
servant to be healed he said, "I do not deserve to
have you come under my roof. That is why I did not
even consider myself worthy to come to you. But say
the word and my servant will be healed. For I myself
am a man under authority with soldiers under me. I
tell this one 'Go' and he goes, and that one 'Come',
and he comes. I say to my servant 'Do this' and he
does it" (Luke 7 6–8). He recognised that the source
of Jesus' authority was that, like him, Jesus was a man
under authority. The centurion might have said, "Like
me you are a man with great authority." Instead, he
saw that Jesus had authority because he was under
authority, just as the centurion's authority came from
being under the authority of the Emperor of Rome.

But there the similarity ends. The authority relationship which Jesus enjoyed with his Father was
not military, it was voluntary. It was not a legalistic
authority, it was, and is, a relational authority. Elsewhere, Jesus indicated that he did only those things
which he saw his Father do and spoke only what he
heard from his Father.

The book of Hebrews explains that "when Christ came into the world he said: 'Sacrifice and offering you did not desire, but a body you prepared for me; with burnt offerings and sin offerings you were not pleased. Then I said . . . I come to do your will, O God.'" (Heb. 10 5–7). In other words God was not satisfied with a legal offering, but desired an obedience born out of responsive relationship. It was not a burden, but a pleasure for Jesus to submit to his Father. The Hebrews passage is quoting from Psalm 40, where the last phrase, in the Authorised Version's translation is: "I delight to do your will, O my God."

When the attacks of the enemy come, the devil will have a field day with us unless we have close and regular fellowship with Christian friends. Unless we have a strong church behind us and come under the authority of its appointed leaders we will be exposed to the enemy.

If you are in ministry of any kind and you are without regular fellowship and are not under any authority or leadership, Satan will get in and destroy you. I have seen it happen with many ministries and it will continue to happen until we are all part of the discipline of the Body of Christ which is his Church.

I hear a lot of rubbish bandied around about being under authority. It mainly comes from people who desire to be in ministry, but are no more than spiritual gypsies, who will not settle under anyone else's care or responsibility. For the other side of the coin of submission is responsibility. The people under whom we place ourselves are not there to be despots, but to care for our souls as those who will have to give account for them.

The buck has to stop somewhere. I am responsible to leaders; they are responsible to the Lord. Ultimately, it is Jesus who takes responsibility because all power has been given to him. But he received power because he showed himself obedient—an obedience which he learned through suffering. In the end the buck stops with Jesus. He is responsible for our ministry, we are responsible to him, but he appoints channels of authority to whom we are answerable. Of course, our loyalty to earthly leaders is always conditional on their faithfulness to the Lord and to the revealed word of God. There is no such thing as unqualified submission, except to Jesus.

Nevertheless, submission is never tested until we are asked to do something with which we do not naturally wish to conform. It is easy to submit when we are required to do something that pleases us anyway. Jesus did not relish the cross, but he went because it was an essential part of his Father's purposes.

The word "authority" has become a dirty word in our homes, in our schools and even in the Church. I believe with all my heart that God has been able to pour out a mighty blessing and an anointing on my preaching because I come under his authority and that of the anointed leaders of our church, which is part of his Body.

Besides giving out to others week after week, I need to take in myself. I receive this intake in the context of a strong and supportive church which has helped me grow in wisdom and in knowledge of the Lord. In addition to these blessings, I have a devoted wife who loves me and who I am learning to love more and more as time goes on. We love our three sons dearly for who they are and what they are in the same way that they love us. The only thing in life that I hate is sin and Satan the author of sin who would seek to break up families and churches in order to rob us of the glory and victory we have in Jesus.

As I look back over the years since Christ found me and claimed me, I am conscious of a security and freedom which I have never known before. The Bible tells us, "It is for freedom that Christ has set us free" (Gal. 5 1). I praise God for proving to me the truth of John chapter 8 verse 36: "If the Son sets you free, you will be free indeed."